Policymaking
in Japan

The Japan Center for International Exchange wishes to thank

Policymaking in Japan

Defining the Role of Politicians

edited by
Gerald L. Curtis

Tokyo • Japan Center for International Exchange • *New York*

The surnames of the authors and other persons mentioned in this book are positioned according to country practice.

Copyediting by Pamela J. Noda.
Cover design by Anne Bergasse, abinitio Y.K.
Design and production by abinitio Y.K.
Cover photographs © Photo Disc Inc.

Printed in Japan
ISBN 4-88907-062-1

Distributed outside Japan by Brookings Institution Press
(1775 Massachusetts Avenue, N.W., Washington, D.C. 20036-2188 U.S.A.)
and Kinokuniya Company Ltd. (5-38-1 Sakuragaoka, Setagaya-ku, Tokyo 156-8691 Japan).

Japan Center for International Exchange
9-17 Minami Azabu 4-chome, Minato-ku, Tokyo 106-0047 Japan
URL: http://www.jcie.or.jp

Japan Center for International Exchange, Inc. (JCIE/USA)
1251 Avenue of the Americas, New York, N.Y. 10020 U.S.A.
URL: http://www.jcie.org

Contents

Foreword

Yamamoto Tadashi

Policymaking in Japan: Defining the Role of Politicians represents the results of a study project on "The Future of Governance and the Role of Politicians," which was directed by Gerald L. Curtis of Columbia University. A major evolution in Japan's system of governance has been taking place in recent years. The relationship between politicians and bureaucrats has been thrown into flux. Redefining that relationship and bringing about fundamental change in the government's policymaking processes and institutions are major challenges facing Japan in these first years of the 21st century.

The chapters in this volume are written by members of the Diet from the Liberal Democratic, Democratic, and New Kōmeitō parties and were first presented as papers at the Global ThinkNet Tokyo Conference held in Japan in November 2001. All the project members participated in the conference, and their papers stimulated a heated debate among other participants, including politicians, policy experts, journalists, and public intellectuals from around the world.

This publication is a sequel to several publications coming out of a series of projects under the core theme of "Globalization, Governance, and Civil Society" that the Japan Center for International Exchange (JCIE) has been pursuing since 1996 in response to a wide array of shifts that became visible in the mid-1990s in civil society, government, politics, and the interaction between those sectors in the face of formidable forces of globalization. Through in-depth examination of the role of civil society in the domestic governance of Japan (*Deciding the Public Good: Governance and Civil Society in Japan,* 1998) and in international governance (*Governance and Civil Society in a Global Age, 2001*), JCIE is focusing on a series of study and dialogue projects considering the health of democracies and prospects for improvement in the conduct of politics and the performance of government. The first project—a comparative study, involving the United States and Japan, jointly organized with the Brookings Institution on how to improve governance, especially focusing on reform—resulted in the publication of *Governance for a New Century: Japanese Challenges, American Experience* (2002). JCIE has also published *Guidance for Governance: Comparing Alternative Sources of Public Policy Advice* (2001), which examined the roles played by alternative policy advisory organizations in a range of democratic countries at different stages of economic and political development. The fact that the members of the Diet themselves wrote the chapters in *Policymaking in Japan* shows how much remains to be done to equip Japanese politicians with enough staff or policy legislative support. It is our hope that these publications, which represent the result of JCIE's policy study projects under its Global ThinkNet Program, will play a useful role in stimulating constructive debate over the critical issues of governance Japan has to grapple with in the coming years.

I would like to express sincere gratitude to the six members of the Diet who participated in this project even under politically difficult and busy circumstances. Special thanks go to Gerald Curtis for his insightful leadership throughout the project. This project and the resulting volume would not have been possible without the generous financial support of the Nippon Foundation, to which JCIE extends its special thanks. I also would like to recognize the invaluable assistance of JCIE staff who worked on this project, especially Suzuki Tomoko and Minorikawa Nobuhide. Finally, I wish to thank Pamela J. Noda, Kim Gould Ashizawa, and Kawaguchi Chie of JCIE for their tireless efforts to ensure that this publication came to fruition.

Yamamoto Tadashi
President
Japan Center for International Exchange

Policymaking
in Japan

1

Politicians and Bureaucrats: What's Wrong and What's to Be Done

Gerald L. Curtis

The following six chapters were written by members of the Diet from the Liberal Democratic, Democratic, and New Kōmeitō parties. They are members of a new generation of politicians in Japan who have a deep interest in issues that affect not just their constituents but the nation as a whole, and who are concerned about designing a new architecture for policymaking.

The six of them participated in a Japan Center for International Exchange study group that I had the pleasure to chair. The study group started out discussing relations between bureaucrats and politicians and how those relations should be restructured. It quickly became evident that the issue of how to restructure the policymaking process involves other questions as well. These include the relationships between the prime minister and the governing party organizations, the role of Diet committees, and the issue of staff support for politicians, parties, the Diet, and the prime minister.

Each of the six chapters that these politicians wrote explores these and other matters of policymaking in the context of a specific policy issue. Each provides important insights into the substantive issue at hand and the policy process relating to it. In this opening chapter, I focus on giving an overview of the issues that currently are of so much concern in Japan related to government policymaking. The chapter discusses why the issue of politician versus bureaucrat draws so much attention in Japan today, what has changed about this relationship in recent years, why further reform of the policymaking process is needed, and what in my view the major objectives of reform should be.

BUREAUCRAT-POLITICIAN COMPETITION

The struggle between politicians and bureaucrats for control over public policy decision making is an important feature of politics in all economically developed countries that have democratic political systems. The father of modern political sociology, the German scholar Max Weber, nearly 100 years ago identified the struggle between bureaucrats who commanded technical expertise and popularly elected politicians who were accountable to the public for the government's policies as potentially one of the most serious challenges to the effective functioning of the democratic political party systems that were then developing in Germany and elsewhere in Europe (see Aberbach et al. 1981).

Many observers of the rising mass democracies in the early 20th century were generally pessimistic about the ultimate outcome of this struggle, believing that as economies became more complex and the need for expertise in making public policy became more pronounced, the bureaucrats' control of information and technical knowledge would give them the upper hand over politicians who were mostly generalists and whose time in office was uncertain. Even the parties themselves, another German sociologist Robert Michels (1956) argued, would become bureaucratized and fall victim to the "iron law of oligarchy."

Weber wrote that skillful bureaucrats do not try to compete openly with politicians for power. They pay lip service to the principle of politician control over the decision-making system and exercise their power by explaining that for technical reasons something the politicians want to do is not feasible or that something the politicians do not want to do is absolutely necessary. And they can sabotage a lot of government policy simply by stalling the implementation of policies of which they do not approve. These insights made so long ago will ring true to anyone familiar with the current Japanese situation.

Beginning this discussion of politician versus bureaucrat in Japan's policy process with a reference to Weber helps to make the point that the Japanese problem is not as unique as many Japanese and many foreign observers of Japan assume it to be. In the United States, there have been many articles and books written about the power of Congressional staffers over the Congressmen they ostensibly serve and about how bureaucrats in line ministries form alliances with the clients of those ministries in the private sector to influence the policy process. The term "iron triangle," which many Japanese use to refer to what they believe is a uniquely incestuous relationship between bureaucrats, industry, and Liberal Democratic Party (LDP) politicians, is a term that originated in the United States to describe the relationship between bureaucrats, industry lobbyists, and members of relevant Congressional committees.

In the United Kingdom, there was a popular television series in the 1980s called "Yes, Minister." The series poked fun at a system in which each morning the new and eager minister calls in his senior bureaucrats and issues his orders for the day. The bureaucrats dutifully say, "Yes, Minister," and leave the room. Later when the minister calls the bureaucrats back in to complain that his orders have not been carried out, the bureaucrats once again obediently say, "Yes, Minister." They leave the room and nothing gets done.* This story has to sound familiar to anyone who is following Prime Minister Koizumi Jun'ichirō's so far unsuccessful efforts to dismantle special public corporations (*tokushu hōjin*) and implement an array of economic reform policies.

In the mid-1970s, I was living in London and working at the Royal Institute for International Affairs (Chatham House). While I was there, I served as moderator of a meeting organized by Chatham House that brought together several British members of parliament (MPs) with a group of Diet members from the Japan Socialist Party (JSP) who were passing through London on their way to attend the British Labour Party convention in Blackpool. The visiting Japanese politicians explained that the LDP's support was steadily and surely declining, that the opposition parties together were close to denying the LDP a majority of seats in the House of Representatives (Lower House), and that the long period of LDP rule would soon come to an end.

After listening to this presentation, the Labour Party MPs at the meeting reminded their Japanese colleagues that when their party first came to power after the Second World War, one of their biggest problems was bureaucratic opposition to anything they tried to do that broke with precedent. If the experience of the United Kingdom and other European countries offered any guide, one MP said with considerable passion, he was sure that when the Socialists came to power they would face a bureaucracy determined to sabotage their policy program.

About a quarter of a century later, I was in a private room at the Hotel New Otani having breakfast with Takemura Masayoshi, the minister of finance in the coalition government of Prime Minister Murayama Tomiichi, the first Socialist to become prime minister. Takemura, like many successful politicians, is a good storyteller and he had many stories to tell of the difficulties he was having getting the bureaucrats in his ministry to

*This BBC television series was later published in book form. See Lynn (1988).

understand that he was in charge and that they were to carry out his orders rather than the other way around.

The bureaucrats, however, kept on insisting that for one technical reason or another, what Takemura wanted to do was infeasible. They also worked hard to isolate the minister politically. At one point, Takemura in frustration said to them that even if what the bureaucrats argued made sense on technical grounds, the political pressures to do what he was insisting upon were simply too great to be denied. At this point, one of the bureaucrats in the meeting with him said that in fact he had visited with former Minister of Finance and Prime Minister Takeshita Noboru just the day before and that Takeshita had expressed agreement with the position the bureaucrats were advocating. Another chimed in that he had had a similar conversation with the head of the Policy Research Council of the LDP, and yet another recounted a similar conversation with a key Socialist Party leader. The bureaucrats had done their *nemawashi*—their behind-the-scenes consultation—with leaders of the political world to isolate their minister. Takemura insisted that he was determined to teach the bureaucrats who was boss and do what he believed was right. Nonetheless, he concluded, he was sure that the bureaucrats would try to find all kinds of ways to sabotage him. We were speaking in Japanese, but he used the English word "sabotage," and when he did so it triggered my memory of the Labour MP's use of the same word in his warning to the Japanese Socialist politicians so many years earlier.

A few days after this breakfast meeting, I was on a bullet train to Nagoya to participate in a public discussion (*taidan*) with another Takemura, this one being Takemura Ken'ichi, a well-known television personality and commentator on current affairs. We had agreed to meet on the train to sketch out what we would talk about at the meeting. No sooner had we sat down than Takemura said that he had had the oddest experience that very morning. A couple of Ministry of Finance (MOF) officials had come to see him to give him some data and other information that they said might be helpful in connection with Minister Takemura's scheduled appearance on his next Sunday morning television show. It was not that unusual, he said, for bureaucrats to do that when their minister was to be interviewed. They would provide information about important issues that the minister was grappling with in the hope that the questioning would take a direction that would enable the minister to publicize the ministry's position and that would reflect well on the minister himself. What was odd about this particular meeting, Takemura said, was that the bureaucrats came armed with materials to show how misguided their minister was in what he was proposing in the way of policy. He pulled out of his attaché case a sheaf of newspaper clippings, data, and other articles that the bureaucrats had left with him, all of which were critical of Minister Takemura. As Takemura had feared would happen, the bureaucrats' effort to sabotage their minister was in full swing, and it involved trying to influence the media as well as the political leadership.

These stories of bureaucrat-politician competition for control over policymaking underscore the point that the Japanese situation is not unique and that there is no simple answer to how to manage this relationship. It is not possible nor is it necessarily desirable simply to put "politicians in charge," which seems to be what the Japanese term *seiji shudō* suggests should be done. Modern democracies need effective bureaucracies staffed with highly skilled experts. To fatally weaken a strong bureaucracy in the name of administrative reform hardly seems a rational thing to do, but a lot of the reform effort in Japan seems to be aimed at doing just that.

Modern democracies also need political accountability, and to achieve that bureaucrats have to be accountable to political leaders, who are the only ones the public can hold accountable for the government's actions. There is no single or simple formula for striking the right balance between bureaucrat and politician. It necessarily differs with each country because of differences in institutions, traditions, and many other factors as well.

It is important not to underestimate the success modern democratic political systems have had in striking an appropriate balance between bureaucratic and politician power. For one thing, the electoral process has proved to be a powerful constraint on bureaucratic power. Political parties and incumbent candidates wanting to win reelection have forced their policy preferences on the bureaucracy whenever they have believed that doing so was necessary for their own political survival. The Japanese government pushed through tax cuts when MOF opposed them. It refused to introduce a consumption tax for at least ten years after MOF first insisted on its necessity, and it resisted raising the tax rate despite MOF demands that it do so. Bureaucrats may try to convince, oppose, and sabotage political leaders. They often are successful. But in the end they lose out to the political leadership when political leaders believe the stakes are high enough to fight for. The Japanese reality is that for so many years when Japan was committed to the national goal of rapid economic growth, politicians believed that what the bureaucrats were doing served their interests and therefore saw little reason to oppose them. Over time, this created a pattern of relations that was comfortable for both politician and bureaucrat. Only now is this relationship being challenged in a significant way.

It is important to correctly identify what precisely the problem is in the relationship between bureaucrat and politician in Japan. A wrong diagnosis is almost certain to produce the wrong prescription for a cure. The conventional wisdom in Japan is that policymaking in the Japanese government is a system of bureaucratic dominance in which politicians have little say except when it comes to pork-barrel types of activities. If the situation were this clear cut, coming up with a rational reform program would not be so difficult. It would involve reducing the power of the bureaucracy and increasing that of the politicians. The situation in Japan, however, is anything but simple and a more nuanced, comprehensive, and bold approach to reform is needed.

The relationship between bureaucrat and politician during the long period of LDP one-party dominance cannot be explained in terms of a zero-sum game in which the bureaucrats had all the power and the politicians had none. Political leaders, not bureaucrats, set the framework for postwar Japanese domestic and foreign policy. When bureaucrats say today—as so many of them do—that they need strong political leadership in order to work effectively, they are not dissembling. The "bureaucracy" is in reality a complex of largely independent, often competing ministries and departments, each with its own policy preferences and goals and none with the ability to establish overarching policy. That is the job of political leaders. It is the failing of political leadership, not the power of the bureaucracy, that is responsible for so many of the problems that Japan currently finds itself facing.

Politicians get deeply involved in micromanaging the policy process. That, after all, is what *zoku giin*—the so-called policy tribes in the LDP that are made up of politicians with specialized knowledge, or at least intense interest, in a particular set of policy issues—do when they use their power to get policy outcomes desired by the private sector interests that support and fund them. A lot of the problems of excessive government spending on wasteful and environmentally damaging public works projects cannot be laid at the door of the bureaucracy; it is politicians who are responsible.

There is an extensive academic literature, mostly in the form of published Ph.D. dissertations by American political scientists who are specialists on Japan, that provides convincing case study evidence of the power of interest groups and politicians on a wide range of public policy decisions. The idea that bureaucrats do everything and politicians do nothing when it comes to policymaking is simply not supported by the empirical data.

At the same time, bureaucrats have enormous power in Japan—arguably more so than in any other modern democratic country. Even France, the closest comparable case to Japan, pales in comparison when it comes to bureaucratic power. Japanese bureaucrats control a great deal of information while politicians have very limited access to information due to the absence of staff support either in the party organizations or among politicians themselves. Information is power and Japanese politicians are heavily dependent on bureaucrats for information, especially given that think tanks and other alternative sources of information and expertise are so weakly developed.

Japanese bureaucrats are protected by stringent civil service laws and by deeply ingrained traditions against political interference in personnel matters. At least until recently, bureaucrats were regarded by the public as being drawn from the best and the brightest the society produced. Bureaucrats were thought to have a sense of mission and a willingness to sacrifice personal material satisfaction to serve the nation, and thus to be incorruptible. For their part, bureaucrats in Japan had a sense of self-confidence and self-importance that goes back to the Meiji period. They came out of a tradition in which those serving in the higher civil service assumed that they, rather than the politicians (much less the masses), were competent to determine public policy. The expression popular in prewar Japan and still well known today, *kanson minpi*—bureaucrats exalted, people despised—captures the essence of this attitude.

Part of the conventional wisdom that Japan has a system of bureaucratic dominance is rooted in the assumption that bureaucrats have expertise and politicians do not. In reality, however, there were many policy experts in the LDP in the past. In its heyday, the LDP drew on two sources for most of its Diet members: policy-wise former high-ranking bureaucrats and street-smart local politicians. The combination was a winning one. The policy experts maintained close ties with bureaucrats in the ministries they themselves came from, and the professional politicians, the *tōjinha*—a term which tellingly has all but disappeared from the Japanese political vocabulary—kept the party's finger on the pulse of the electorate and gave it its populist appeal. In this system the bureaucracy functioned as a powerful and respected think tank for the ruling party.

Today this combination has disappeared. Former bureaucrats entering politics now usually do so after only a relatively brief career in the bureaucracy. They do not have the extensive experience and contacts that earlier generations of bureaucrats-turned-politicians commanded. The professional machine politicians also are far fewer in number, especially now that so many Diet members are second-generation politicians with no experience in elective politics before running for the seat vacated by their father or other close relative.

Moreover, whereas policy experts in the LDP in the past saw their task as working hand in glove with the bureaucrats (who in many cases were the former subordinates of the men now running the LDP) to effect a broadly shared vision of national goals and a common understanding of policy priorities, today there is no such vision and no broad-based consensus on what those priorities should be. The system was so successful for so long that over time many LDP politicians came to take it for granted that the bureaucracy would be able to design the kinds of policies that would make Japan prosperous and keep the LDP in power. Now Japan is in economic trouble and the LDP can only stay in power by forming a coalition with other parties. It is not surprising that the politicians want to blame the bureaucrats.

CHANGING PUBLIC ATTITUDES

The issue of bureaucrat versus politician is important in Japan today not because bureaucrats have had all the power but because fundamental social change, shifting popular values, basic structural changes in the political system, and new social needs have undermined a policymaking system that functioned well for many years in the past. Many LDP politicians seem bewildered by the fact that positions they have taken for years that were popular with their constituents are now suddenly deeply unpopular. To a truly remarkable degree, many of them seem unaware how much Japanese society has changed, especially in the past decade. This change is true not only for urban areas but for rural Japan as well. The ability of local elites to deliver the vote has declined markedly. Former Prime Minister Hashimoto Ryūtarō made that painful discovery in the 2001 LDP presidential election when the party machinery and its supporting interest groups proved unable to deliver the vote to him and prevent Koizumi's victory.

Public attitudes toward government spending on public works are a good example of how social change has affected the dynamic of politics.

Japan's most popular prime minister since the Second World War is the current prime minister, Koizumi. Before him, the most popular was the leader of the anti-LDP coalition that came to power in 1993, Hosokawa Morihiro. Prior to that, however, postwar Japan's most popular prime minister was the godfather of Japan's public works spending programs, Tanaka Kakuei.

Tanaka's plan was to "remodel the Japanese archipelago," in large part by undertaking a huge incomes transfer policy that took taxes paid by people in urban Japan and gave that money to people living in rural Japan primarily through spending on public works. This plan was enormously popular with Japanese, both urban and rural. Many urban dwellers, after all, were themselves migrants from rural Japan, drawn to the city to work in the industries that were fueling Japan's rapid economic growth. When Tanaka called for policies to raise the living standards of people on the Japan Sea side of the country and elsewhere in poor regions, urban people responded positively. They had sentimental ties to their own *furusato*, or rural hometown, and felt affluent enough to support this kind of policy. Public works projects were popular.

Today, attitudes are very different. Most urban dwellers no longer have close ties to rural Japan. Consequently, the idea that money should be taken from people in the cities and spent on public works in the countryside, especially in a difficult economic environment, now enrages the public where a couple of decades ago they applauded it. That is why Koizumi's pledge to reduce public works spending is as much a source of his popularity today as the pledge to increase it was a source of Tanaka's support 30 years ago. Bureaucrats and politicians have vested interests in perpetuating the system that Tanaka perfected, however, and their resistance to change is fierce.

Japanese society today is characterized by pluralistic competing public demands on government resources, by a civil society that seeks greater autonomy from the state, and by an economy that can look forward to low growth at best. In such an environment there is a pressing need to set new priorities and to make hard choices—tasks that bureaucracies are notably ill-designed to undertake successfully. Interdepartmental, much less interministerial coordination is difficult to achieve in complex bureaucratic organizations, and a bias in favor of following precedent greatly reduces the bureaucracy's ability to respond flexibly to new social needs.

In the absence of a concerted effort to restructure the policymaking system in a way that responds to current needs, Japan will simply drift as if on automatic pilot without direction or purpose. Given the seriousness of the problems Japan confronts in respect not only to the economy and financial system but in terms of social policy and, in the aftermath of September 11, foreign and security policy as well, a failure to fundamentally reform the policymaking system is fraught with dangers.

The issue of politician versus bureaucrat has become especially salient in Japan today because of the public's loss of confidence in the bureaucracy. The 1990s is often referred to as a "lost decade" for Japan, and it certainly was that in many ways. But it was also a watershed decade for Japan, one in which values and attitudes that for a long time characterized Japan changed dramatically. Women's attitudes about marriage and work for example, attitudes of youth about the accomplishments and failures of their parents' generation, or public attitudes about opening the country to foreign imports and investment are remarkably different from what they were before the 1990s. And one of the most dramatic historical changes in recent Japanese history has been the rise of antibureaucrat sentiment and of a kind of antielitism more generally among the Japanese public.

The traditional image of the Japanese bureaucracy as incorruptible, competent, and trustworthy has suffered irreparable damage as a result of policy failures and scandals that have hit one ministry after another since the early 1990s. The Ministry of Health and Welfare was rocked by a nursing home kickback scandal involving its vice minister and by public outrage at that ministry's failure to adequately monitor the import of blood products, leading to the infection with the HIV virus of a large number of the hemophiliac population in Japan. The MOF produced a series of corruption scandals and its policy failures in the aftermath of the collapse of the bubble economy undercut its image for competence. Gross corruption among officials of the Ministry of Foreign Affairs who created a secret slush fund through kickbacks from companies hired to provide services for the ministry was greeted with anger by the public and with cheers for Foreign Minister Tanaka Makiko's decision to purge some of the ministry's most senior officials. The most recent scandal involved the Ministry of Agriculture, Forestry and Fisheries which, despite knowing for the past 15 years from the experience of the United Kingdom that ground bone meal was potentially a source of mad cow disease, continued to allow the importation of such feed products until the disease showed up in Japan in the fall of 2001. The sense that Agriculture Ministry bureaucrats were more concerned about the economic well-being of the beef producers in the country than they were with the public's welfare only reinforced an already strong view that the bureaucracy could not be trusted to act in the national interest. This change in public attitudes amounts to a fundamental change in Japan's political culture. It is something from which the bureaucracy will never be able fully to recover.

The Japanese bureaucracy has been weakened in other ways as well. In the early postwar years, bureaucrats who retired to enter politics generally did so after reaching very high positions in their ministries. They came into politics with many years of experience, expertise, loyal subordinates left behind, and extensive ties with leaders in the private sector. Today, those bureaucrats who enter politics invariably do so early in their careers, at least in the more important Lower House. They are in effect giving up a bureaucratic career in favor of a political one. They have neither the extensive webs of personal relationships nor the rich experience that former generations of bureaucrat-politicians had. Many of them are very talented, but their role has to be fundamentally different from that played by politicians who in the past came into politics after a long bureaucratic career.

Bureaucratic power is also being challenged in a new way by changing public attitudes about transparency and accountability. These issues did not seem so important to the Japanese public as long as a consensus on economic growth prevailed and government policy successfully pursued the grand national project of catching up with the West. Transparency and accountability are perceived very differently today. Both the Japanese public and global markets want to see reforms in Japan to reduce the discretionary authority of bureaucrats and the pattern of informal collusion between bureaucrats and their industry sector clients in favor of a more transparent, rules-based system of far more limited state power. Prime Minister Koizumi's popularity derives in part from his promise to dismantle a lot of the state apparatus in the form of privatizing and eliminating special public corporations, reducing public works spending, and bringing about more extensive deregulation. The Japanese bureaucracy cannot recover its former position of eminence, and politicians are trying to find a way to fill the vacuum its decline has produced.

The other factor that makes the issue of politician versus bureaucrat so important in Japan today, and that makes it so different an issue than in the past, is the change that has occurred in the political system itself. One-party dominance ended in 1993. Japan has had coalition governments ever since, and there is every reason to believe that it will continue to have coalition governments for the foreseeable future. For as long as the LDP was the only governmental party, there was stability in the relationship between party and bureaucracy. Since 1993, that relationship has been in considerable flux.

During the Hosokawa administration, the vice minister of the MOF openly aligned himself with Ozawa Ichirō to try to force an increase in the consumption tax to 7 percent under the guise of changing it to a "social welfare" tax. In the process, he brought down a torrent of criticism on MOF for its overt interference in the political process. Hosokawa tried to innovate a new policymaking process since he had to gain the support of seven coalition parties to get anything approved, but his government, and that of his short-lived successor Hata Tsutomu, fell before a new system could be established.

Then, under the three-party coalition government of Prime Minister Murayama, there was a significant increase in the power of party organizations, such as the LDP Policy Research Council, in coordinating policy among the three parties. The requirements of coalition government greatly weakened long-existing patterns of policymaking. The role of *kokutai* politics—the behind-the-scenes collusion between the LDP and the opposition parties to move the legislative agenda forward—sharply declined as party leaders shifted their attention to getting agreement among the parties in power rather than working out private deals with the opposition.

Under Prime Minister Hashimoto, the effort was made to strengthen and to shift power more to the Prime Minister's Office, the *kantei*. One of the important reforms Hashimoto introduced, which first came into effect a couple of years after he left office, was to strengthen the *kantei*, streamline the bureaucracy, and introduce a new system of senior vice ministers and parliamentary secretaries, all of which was intended to reduce bureaucratic power and increase the power of the prime minister.

Developments since the early 1990s in the policymaking system, however, have exacerbated compeititon between the *kantei* and executives of the ruling parties for control over policy decisions. Policymaking always has involved coordinated action among the prime minister and his cabinet, the ruling party, and the bureaucracy. Now, however, a veritable dual power structure has emerged. Since Prime Minister Koizumi has committed himself to implement reforms that many people in his own party oppose, LDP leaders have used the party's decision-making organs to thwart his reform drive. They have tried, for example, to use certain customary practices, such as the tradition of having all cabinet bills approved by the LDP before they are submitted to the Diet, to prevent the prime minister from moving forward with his reform program. Whether Koizumi wins this battle over control of policy decision making for the *kantei* will have a major impact on how successful he will be in carrying out his reform program and on whether a new *kantei*- and cabinet-centered decision making process will be created.

The old policymaking system no longer functions effectively and a new one has not yet been consolidated. The *kantei* has increased its powers but it has not established its control over policymaking. There is a new policy-mindedness among younger politicians, the so-called *seisaku shinjinrui*, but their involvement in the policy process is limited and ad hoc. The system of senior vice ministers is not likely to have a major positive impact on policymaking. Since these vice ministers have no personal staff of their own, they are entirely reliant on the bureaucrats they ostensibly lead for their information. This system essentially increases the number of politician spokesmen for bureaucratic policy positions and gives the bureaucracy a chance to "educate" a larger number of politicians than in the past on how to think about issues.

Moreover, while Prime Minister Koizumi insisted on appointing cabinet ministers without regard to factional politics, he has left the choice of senior vice ministers and parliamentary secretaries to the party secretary-general. Factional considerations dominate these appointments and they make it difficult for the minister and his vice minister and parliamentary secretary to operate as a coordinated strategy team.

Koizumi has tried to change the cabinet culture, but so far he has had only limited success. In Japan, the cabinet has traditionally been a body of collective leadership rather than one committed to carrying out the prime minister's program. Many cabinet ministers have seen their job as representing the interests of their ministry, meaning interests as defined by ministry bureaucrats, rather than imposing thc demands of the prime minister on the bureaucrats under their charge.

Koizumi's promise to change these traditional assumptions and practices and to strengthen his cabinet ministers' control over their ministries' career bureaucrats seemed to be betrayed by his decision to sack his popular foreign minister, Tanaka Makiko, in February 2002. Tanaka was popular precisely because she was a fearless and forceful critic of the bureaucracy and committed to reforming the foreign office. After the administrative vice minister decided to ban two Japan-based nongovernmental organizations (NGOs) from participating in the International Conference on Reconstruction Assistance to Afghanistan, held in Tokyo in January 2002, apparently in response to pressure from a powerful LDP politician and without consulting the foreign minister, Tanaka ordered the decision reversed. This led to a public argument with Tanaka on one side and the LDP politician, Suzuki Muneo, and the administrative vice minister on the other, about whether the vice minister had told Tanaka that Suzuki had demanded that the NGOs be banned.

Koizumi's decision to end the matter by removing both Tanaka and the vice minister, and having Suzuki resign his position as chair of an important Diet committee, was greeted with outrage by the public and produced a freefall in Koizumi's popularity ratings. The incident could hardly have been worse for the prime minister, since it called into question his commitment to reform the political and governmental system, which was precisely the plank in his program that the public found most appealing.

DESIGNING A NEW POLICYMAKING SYSTEM

So what is to be done? Weakening a bureaucracy that has many strengths and increasing the power of politicians does not on the face of it necessarily suggest that better policy will result. The situation could become much worse. Under the current electoral system, most members of the Lower House are elected in small, single-member districts in which personal support rather than party organizational power is the key to political success. Such a system is tailor-made for politicians who focus on locality-specific, pork-barrel type activities. Simply increasing the power of politicians in this system could produce pressures for public spending that would exacerbate rather than reverse patterns of political behavior that are the source of so much criticism today.

Nonetheless, there is a clear need to innovate a system that gives politicians a greater role in designing policy. Politicians and bureaucrats have different roles to play, but it seems unrealistic and undesirable to say that the politicians' role should be limited to setting the overall framework for and goals of policy, and that the bureaucrats' role should be to make policy to achieve those goals. Politicians need to be directly involved in making policy, and they need access to the expertise—bureaucratic and otherwise—that makes that possible.

Frustration with the difficulties of designing a new policymaking system has led many politicians and commentators to favor constitutional revision to provide for the direct election of the prime minister. In my view, such a reform is likely to prove disastrous. Party identification is extraordinarily weak in Japan—far weaker than in any other democratic country. A direct election of the prime minister would be an election centered entirely on personality and would have little if any base in party organization and identification. That only increases the possibility that the election would become a contest between candidates who are personally popular for reasons that may not be relevant at all to the task of governing a nation. The dangers that such a system would produce a populist leader, in the very worst sense of that term, would be very great. So, too, is the danger that the directly elected prime minister would not have the support of the majority of the parliament, or that parties would fragment in response to the introduction of this system, as happened in Israel. As long as Japan has a parliamentary system, it is better off doing the only thing that makes sense in parliamentary systems, which is to have the individual who can obtain the support of the majority of the members of the parliament become prime minister and form a cabinet.

There is growing agreement among Japanese political observers and among younger Japanese politicians that the single most important policymaking system reform needed is a strengthening of the *kantei* and the powers of the prime minister. This is the goal as well of those who argue for the direct election of the prime minister, but in Japan's parliamentary system it makes more sense to achieve it by strengthening the policymaking capabilities of the *kantei* and ending a system in which leaders in the ruling party play a central role in policymaking. In principle, party decision-making organs should function as a kind of shadow cabinet when the party is in opposition, but they should not be important policymaking bodies when the party is in power.

There is a parallel need for radical reform of the Diet and the strengthening of its role in policymaking. This, too, involves shifting power from the ruling party's organization to the institution that the Constitution defines as the supreme organ of state power, the Diet. In the Japanese parliament, unlike the U.S. Congress, party discipline is almost total. Party members vote as their leadership directs almost without exception. The great preponderance of bills, as is true for all parliamentary systems, are cabinet bills. Yet Japanese election campaigns are very much personality-centered affairs in which candidates make a great deal out of telling the voters what they as individual Diet members will do in terms of policy if elected. It has always puzzled me why voters do not find these kind of campaign speeches ridiculous since, once elected, the backbenchers vote exactly as their party orders.

There is something to be said for defining a new functional division between the *kantei* and a strengthened Diet committee structure that would give more power to Diet committees to write legislation, and that would suspend party discipline on voting on member bills. This would invigorate the Diet and would get politicians to show up at the Diet early in the morning rather than at the party's Policy Research Council.

It probably also makes sense to modernize parliamentary rules, many of which go back to the early years of the 20th century. One such change would be to establish a system in which the party or parties in a coalition that had control of the government also controlled the chairmanships and majorities of Diet committees. Under the Japanese system, a simple majority of seats does not give the ruling parties such majorities. Opposition parties have the chairmanship of some committees in the Diet today, which only obfuscates issues of accountability. On a somewhat more technical level, the system of *innai kaiha*—a caucus system in which parties that remain separate as electoral parties form unified caucuses in the Diet—also is in need of reform. This system, too, obscures issues of accountability and leads to opportunistic arrangements in order to get committee chairmanships, longer question time, the right to submit bills, and so on (Curtis 2000).

To make any meaningful reform program work necessarily involves increasing politicians' access to expertise. A system in which parties and individual Diet members had competent policy staff that transferred to positions as Diet committee staff when their party was in power would not eliminate the role of bureaucrats as experts, but it would insert a group of experts loyal to the politicians and parties (rather than to the ministries) between the elected political leadership and the professional bureaucracy.

One can argue over the details, but the point I wish to make is that reform of the policy process in Japan has two essential elements: eliminating the dual structure of government-ruling party power in favor of a concentration of power in the prime minister and cabinet, and making the Diet a center for policymaking and not just policy approval.

There is little reason to be optimistic, however, that such reforms will be adopted. The inertia created by tradition, the vested interests that would be threatened by radical reform, and even public opposition to spending the tax money that would be needed to provide the kind of staffing required by parties and politicians all act as obstacles to reform. Yet, as we see from reading the chapters prepared for this volume by politicians who represent the best of the new generation, there is a growing number of people in the Diet who are keenly aware of the need to change the system by which government decisions are made. Each of these chapters points to the need to strengthen the prime minister's leadership and the Diet's legislative role. The weakness of these institutions, it seems, is the nub of the problem, and more radical reform than has yet been contemplated in Japan to strengthen these institutions is what needs to be instituted.

BIBLIOGRAPHY

Aberbach, Joel, et al., eds. 1981. *Bureaucrats and Politicians in Western Democracies.* Cambridge, Mass.: Harvard University Press.

Curtis, Gerald L. 2000. *The Logic of Japanese Politics.* New York, N.Y.: Columbia University Press.

Lynn, Jonathan. 1988. *Yes, Prime Minister: The Diaries of the Right Hon. James Hacker.* Topsfield, Mass.: Salem House.

Michels, Robert. 1956. *Political Parties: A Sociological Study of the Oligarchical Tendencies of Modern Democracies.* Glencoe, Ill.: Free Press.

2

The Successful Handling of the Financial Crisis

Nemoto Takumi

For many years now, people in Japan have been calling for the introduction of *seiji shudō*, a politically dominated system where elected politicians would take the lead in making public policy. There has been some progress in recent years toward that objective. Along with the organizational overhaul of the central government that was implemented in January 2001, a new system was introduced under which legislators serve as senior vice ministers and parliamentary secretaries in all cabinet-level ministries and agencies. But this system remains in the trial-and-error stage, and we still lack a system of clear leadership by politicians in this country. In this chapter, I will introduce my own experiences as one member of the Diet who has tried to play a leading role in policymaking, particularly in response to the financial crisis that struck Japan in the late 1990s, and I will attempt to draw conclusions for further reforms to strengthen the ability of politicians to fulfill their responsibilities as policymakers.

I started my own career as a politician in 1993, running in the July general election as a candidate of the ruling Liberal Democratic Party (LDP). Although I personally succeeded in winning a seat in the House of Representatives (Lower House), on the whole my party fared badly in that election. As a result, the LDP fell from power for the first time in nearly four decades. My parliamentary debut was thus as a member of the opposition.

The fall of the LDP brought an end to the so-called 1955 system,[1] under which the bureaucrats drafted policy proposals and then took them to the LDP's Policy Research Council for approval, relying on the political power of the LDP to secure passage of the legislation required to implement the policies. This arrangement, however, was predicated on the LDP being the party in power. The bureaucrats have a strong tendency to see the members of the ruling party or parties as their allies, and so they started keeping their distance from the Liberal Democrats as soon as the LDP fell from power. Since the party had until then relied on the bureaucracy as its source of policy ideas, the veteran LDP legislators were suddenly at a complete loss.

Having just been elected, however, I had no experience with the previous system. I believed that my mission as an elected representative was to listen to the voices of my constituents and to turn their input into concrete policies. So I plunged right in, trying to overcome the handicap of being in the opposition and find ways to formulate policy proposals and get them approved from my position outside the government. That position shifted less than a year later when the LDP returned to power, this time as the senior partner in a ruling coalition. Short though it was, however, my experience as an opposition legislator was valuable, teaching me the limits of the bureaucracy-dominated system of policymaking.

The experience also proved invaluable three years later, as my colleagues and I attempted to respond to the financial panic of late 1997—a critical situation requiring politically led policymaking. The traditional bureaucracy-dominated system was incapable of dealing with this emergency, and consequently the policymaking initiative fell into the hands of junior legislators—myself included.

In the late summer and autumn of 1998, as efforts to deal with the crisis came to a head, media attention focused on the major role being played by the younger legislators. People dubbed us the *seisaku shinjinrui*, a term that might be literally translated as the "new breed of policymakers." In the following section, I will examine the emergence of this new breed of activist legislator.

THE SHIFT FROM BUREAUCRATIC TO POLITICAL DOMINANCE

As I have noted, the July 1993 Lower House election resulted in the defeat of the LDP, which was forced to yield power to an eight-way coalition of anti-LDP forces. Over the 38 years of the 1955 system, however, the LDP had developed a close policymaking partnership with the bureaucracy, which the party used in effect as its own think tank. Through this partnership, successive LDP administrations had succeeded in turning Japan into the world's second-largest economic power.

This arrangement functioned smoothly as long as the Liberal Democrats were properly aware of their responsibility for policy and there was an appropriate degree of orderliness and tension in the relationship between them and the bureaucrats on whom they relied for policymaking assistance. But over the course of time, the politicians gradually relaxed their hold on the reins, and in a number of crucial fields—such as financial regulation—they came to rely completely on the bureaucrats. Thus it was that a bureaucracy-dominated system was allowed to take root.

The process of drafting and implementing policy must be accompanied by discipline and responsibility. The emergence of the system of bureaucratic dominance was the fault of the Liberal Democratic politicians who allowed the bureaucrats to take control. So the defeat of the LDP in 1993 represented a good chance to correct the situation. And the new administration that was inaugurated that August under Prime Minister Hosokawa Morihiro, the popular leader of the Japan New Party, proclaimed that it would bring the bureaucrats' power under control. But the new ruling coalition, which was comprised of eight relatively small parties, ended up relying even more heavily on the bureaucracy than had the LDP. Perhaps the most egregious example was a proposal for a new "national welfare tax," which was drawn up by the bureaucrats of the powerful Ministry of Finance and was adopted by the Hosokawa administration without any serious review by the members of the Diet.

In April 1994, Hosokawa resigned and a new coalition was formed under Hata Tsutomu, head of the Japan Renewal Party. But Hata's coalition did not even have a clear legislative majority, and it was incapable of exerting control over the bureaucracy. It fell barely two months after its inauguration, and the LDP returned to power, this time in a coalition with the Socialists and a third small party.

The bureaucracy's strength lies in its store of policymaking expertise and its effective monopoly on much of the necessary information. In order to seize the policy reins from the bureaucrats' grip, politicians must possess a combination of strengths of their own: logic, wisdom, a sense of balance, conceptual power, and the power of persuasion. Having started out on the opposition side in the Diet, I was strongly conscious of this set of requirements, and I worked at building my own capabilities in those areas where I felt I was lacking. At the same time, I actively cooperated with other junior legislators in producing policy recommendations, and together we were able to get a number of our proposals implemented. On the basis of this track record, we were beginning to earn a reputation within the LDP as policy crafters. Then, the Japanese economy was shaken by a huge tremor, the financial panic of November 1997.

Beginning that month, a number of financial institutions went under in rapid succession: Sanyō Securities, Hokkaido Takushoku Bank, Yamaichi Securities (one of the big four brokerage houses), and Tokuyō City Bank. The direct cause of this chain reaction was the default on obligations in the call market (the overnight interbank money market) that occurred immediately after the collapse of Sanyō Securities. If the financial authorities (specifically, the mandarins of the Banking Bureau within the Ministry of Finance) had properly gauged the gravity of the situation when the default occurred and had acted to prevent its recurrence, the ensuing rush of bankruptcies might have been averted, along with the runs on certain banks by panicky depositors. At the time, however, it was all the bureaucrats could do just to deal with the individual cases of bankruptcy as they happened. This inability to take preventive action and defuse the crisis highlighted the limits of the bureaucracy-dominated system, which became totally ineffective during the subsequent debate over infusions of public funds to shore up financial institutions.

The reason Japan's financial sector malfunctioned so severely was the delay in dealing with the problem of nonperforming loans. Shortly after the November 1997 panic, politicians took the lead in planning and implementing injections of capital from the public sector into the major banks. Unfortunately, however, this did not produce a fundamental solution to the problem. The only way to deal effectively with financial institutions' nonperforming loans is to get them off the balance sheets.

Many of the loans that had gone sour had been made with real estate as collateral. Many of us in the LDP believed that if ownership of such real estate were more easily transferable, banks would be able to sell off the properties they had taken as collateral and thereby wipe the bad loans off their books. This, we thought, would allow the financial sector to recover.

It was with this idea in mind that the LDP, which had assumed the policy reins from the paralyzed mandarins of the Ministry of Finance (MOF), started to prepare measures in February 1998 to promote the liquidity of land and financial credits. The work was undertaken by a special committee to promote the Comprehensive Plan for Financial Revitalization (known as the Total Plan), which was headed by Yasuoka Okiharu. The core members were Ishihara Nobuteru (now minister of state for administrative reform and regulatory reform), Shiozaki Yasuhisa, and me. A number of other junior and mid-ranking legislators also took part, including Watanabe Yoshimi.

The fact that we younger Diet members were assigned this important job was due to our having previously served in policymaking posts within the party. Junior legislators, however talented, cannot put their abilities to work unless they are assigned to positions of responsibility. In this respect, we owed much to the understanding of two senior figures within the party—Katō Kōichi, who at the time was the LDP's secretary-general, and Yamasaki Taku, who headed the party's Policy Research Council. They have both consistently called for a change of generations within the party's organization.

Our committee worked intensively on this project, taking the policymaking initiative firmly into our own hands. Within a two-month period, we were able to complete work on the Total Plan for Increased Liquidity of Land and Credits, which was incorporated into the package of emergency economic measures set forth by the LDP toward the end of April that year. Often in Japan, multiple financial institutions and other creditors have claims on a single piece of land. These overlapping claims need to be sorted out before the land can be sold in settlement of an unpaid loan. Our plan was designed to make it possible to break through this logjam and get the property on the market.

Our next step was to come up with a scheme that would push financial institutions to effectively dispose of their nonperforming credits, get the financial system on the road to recovery, and promote structural reform. Unfortunately, as we were undertaking this new task, the extent of the crisis facing the Long-Term Credit Bank of Japan (LTCB) came to light, making our work even more difficult than it otherwise would have been. But this also gave us a strong sense of urgency, and so we stepped up the pace of our politically dominated initiative and were able to get approval on July 2 for our second "total plan," the Comprehensive Plan for Financial Revitalization.

In our work to develop these plans, we started out by sketching the overall policy outline. Next we conducted repeated and thorough consultations with representatives of the responsible bureaucratic organs. We considered this feedback and then put together the final drafts of the plans. I believe that this is a successful example of the politically dominated approach that Japan requires: we adopted an appropriate form of policymaking with elected politicians taking the lead.

Japan has many highly capable bureaucrats. But there are limits to what they can successfully handle, and naturally they cannot be expected to make political judgments. Because their perspective is that of their particular ministry or agency, it is difficult for them to coordinate their views on policy topics that cut across organizational lines or that involve important issues of overall national strategy.

The Cabinet Councillors' Office on Internal Affairs does exist within the bureaucracy to serve as a policy coordination organ, but all it really manages to do is assemble proposals from the various ministries and agencies and package them to look like a comprehensive policy set. One bureaucratic organ cannot really be expected to negotiate the conflicting pulls of individual policies from other bureaucratic organs and merge them all together into a coherent whole. As a result, it is up to politicians to deal with the formulation of policy in areas that involve multiple agencies or matters of national strategy. My own involvement in the policymaking process made me recognize even more strongly than before just how important it is for elected politicians to exercise leadership in this respect.

To accomplish this, politicians naturally must have the requisite policymaking knowledge. Ishihara, Shiozaki, and I—who formed the nucleus of the junior legislator policymaking team—met this requirement, each in our own way. Ishihara had been actively involved in fiscal and monetary policy affairs ever since becoming a national legislator. Shiozaki was an expert on finance, having worked for years at the Bank of Japan (BOJ). And I, having begun my career as a bureaucrat in the Ministry of Construction, was familiar with the policymaking process. I did not have any specialized knowledge of finance, but I studied diligently to overcome that shortcoming. The three of us, together with other energetic and eager Diet members of our generation, developed and refined our policy proposals through a rigorous brainstorming process.

It was unprecedented for this sort of crucial policymaking agenda to be entrusted to a group of relatively junior Diet members like us. It had become possible in part because the power of the bureaucracy had declined, making it easier for politicians to take the policy reins. But the biggest factor was the collapse of the 1955 system—and with it the structure of control by the LDP elders—which threw the political world into disorder. The result was the assignment of important work to younger legislators who were eager to practice policy-centered politics.

The two Total Plans that we put together proved that it was possible for politicians to take the lead in formulating important policies. They also served as a model of politically dominated policymaking in terms of the close teamwork that we achieved between the cabinet and the ruling party. In addition, the policymaking process benefited from the smooth interaction between Prime Minister Hashimoto Ryūtarō and LDP Secretary-General Katō, both of whom were policy experts in their own right.

When we were putting together the second Total Plan, we expected that the LDP would emerge victorious from the House of Councillors (Upper House) election held on July 12, 1998. According to the scenario we envisioned, an extraordinary Diet session would then be convened toward the end of July and it would enact the government's package of six laws for financial revitalization no later than mid-August. We believed that quick action was essential to defuse the financial crisis.

However, the LDP unexpectedly suffered a major defeat in the Upper House election, and our schedule was greatly disrupted as a result. At the subsequent extraordinary Diet session that deliberated the financial crisis, the opposition parties presented a joint legislative proposal in competition with the one presented by the ruling party, and the Diet became bogged down in the struggle between the two sides.[2] As the deliberations dragged on, the share price of the troubled LTCB dropped again, which further aggravated concerns about the stability of the financial system.

As the situation appeared to be descending into a vicious cycle, junior legislators from the LDP and from the opposition Democratic Party of Japan entered into talks to reach a compromise. Based on those negotiations, the original LDP package was revised and two key laws were passed in October: the Financial Revitalization Law, which stipulated procedures for handling the failure of financial institutions, and the Financial Function Early Strengthening Law, which provided for up to ¥60 trillion in public funds to be used in shoring up banks' capital adequacy.

Politicians also took the initiative on the LTCB issue. Instead of trying to find a solution under previously existing legislation, it was decided that the troubled bank would be dealt with under the new Financial Revitalization Law. As soon as the new law went into effect, it was applied to the LTCB, which was temporarily placed under government ownership.

As I have outlined here, the process in which the 1997 financial crisis was addressed involved a politically dominated system centering on younger legislators. This took place against the backdrop of a rapid decline in the power of the bureaucracy, which had previously been in effective control of the financial sector, and the resulting shift of initiative to the hands of elected politicians. In putting together the best set of policies we could within the limited time available, we fully and unhesitatingly called on experts in the bureaucracy for assistance—particularly in negotiations with the Cabinet Legislation Bureau over the legislative package and in dealing with the parts of the proposed legislation that required specialized technical knowledge. Some people have suggested that such an approach might invite a return to the old bureaucracy-dominated system. But there is no danger of this happening if, as I noted at the beginning of this chapter, politicians are aware of their responsibility for policy and maintain an appropriate degree of orderliness and tension in their relationship with the bureaucrats who assist them. For the politically dominated system to work effectively, politicians must be able to exercise their leadership both by thinking for themselves and by making full use of bureaucratic resources and expertise.

PRESCRIPTIONS FOR ECONOMIC REVIVAL: THE THREE TOTAL PLANS

The implementation of the pair of Total Plans that I have mentioned allowed Japan to weather the financial crisis that struck in 1997. In this section, I will offer an outline of those plans, as well as a third comprehensive set of proposals that my colleagues and I have formulated, the Survival Plan for the Japanese Economy.

Total Plan for Increased Liquidity of Land and Credits

In our first set of proposed policies, the Total Plan for Increased Liquidity of Land and Credits, we provided a set of four major measures designed to work comprehensively from start to finish of the process of increasing the liquidity of land and audits. First, it set forth clear measures to smooth the handling of relationships between creditors and debtors. We proposed concrete steps that included the improvement of the auction system, the opening up of the "servicer" business (debt-collection activities that had previously been limited to lawyers), and the establishment of real estate rights adjustment committees to clear up the complex web of land rights. In addition, for the first time in Japan we introduced the concept of "due diligence"—which is applied as a matter of course in Western countries—to the task of assessing the current value of collateral real estate for bad loans and determining the amount of the outstanding credit that cannot be recovered.

In line with our proposal to allow the operation of debt-collection activities by private sector businesses, a Servicer Law (Law Regarding

Special Measures Regarding Debt Collection Business) was enacted in October 1998. As of the end of 2001, some 50 debt-collection agencies that have been established under this law have handled roughly ¥36 trillion in debts, and have already collected approximately ¥1.4 billion.

We also called for the expansion of the functions of the Cooperative Credit Purchasing Company, which buys the credit obligations (with real estate as security) of financial companies such as banks and then sells the real estate, including the commencement of bulk sales and the strengthening of efforts to sell off collateral real estate, thanks to which this organization's collection rate has improved substantially over the past three years, rising from 30 percent in fiscal year 1998 to 80 percent in fiscal 2000.

In addition, we proposed the enactment of a Law on Securitization of Specified Assets by Special Purpose Companies (SPC Law) to facilitate the sale of nonperforming assets by issuing small-denomination securities that are managed by firms set up for that purpose.

The second major measure involved the larger objective of the promotion of urban redevelopment through measures to redraw property lines and consolidate small plots of land so as to put together reasonably sized and shaped development sites. Here the main idea was to make use of the Housing and Urban Development Corporation (called the Urban Development Corporation since October 1999), which had originally been formed after World War II to both sell and rent good housing at low cost. The corporation was subsequently provided with ¥300 billion in public funds as additional equity.

The third measure was the creation of public-sector demand for land to use in urban redevelopment. This was centered around national subsidies that aimed at generating demand for land through a comprehensive set of policies in such areas as welfare, disaster prevention, housing, and the revitalization of commercial districts. The intention here is to foster community growth and activate local economies through the purchase of land by the public sector for urban redevelopment.

And fourth, we proposed the improvement of the system of rehabilitation-oriented handling of corporate failures. The existing Composition Law and Corporate Rehabilitation Law were both oriented toward rehabilitation, but the former required companies to be bankrupt before it could be applied, while the latter was designed with large corporations in mind and the process of drafting a rehabilitation plan was excessively time-consuming. Both laws entailed cumbersome procedures, and neither offered a viable approach for a wide range of corporations in trouble.

We therefore called for the urgent enactment of legislation to provide for rehabilitation-oriented procedures that companies could use before becoming insolvent to facilitate their prompt rehabilitation. We suggested, for example, that Japan should refer to the Chapter 11 procedures of U.S. law in this connection. The Ministry of Justice heeded our call for urgent action, and this led to the enactment of the Civil Rehabilitation Law in December 1999.

One additional feature of this plan was that we included explicit time frames for all of the proposed measures, ranging from the clarification of the bad-debt situation through the effective use of collateral real estate and the stimulation of the real estate market. In this way, we tried to ensure that the proposals would be acted upon rather than remaining as mere blueprints.

Comprehensive Plan for Financial Revitalization

As the second stage of our program to fundamentally resolve the bad-loan problem, we proposed a total plan for revitalization of the financial sector, formally titled the Comprehensive Plan for Financial Revitalization. With this, we offered an overall set of prescriptions aimed at structural reform of the financial system. The plan included the following concrete measures designed to promote the rationalization and regrouping of financial institutions:

(1) disclosure of nonperforming assets, write-offs of bad debts, and maintenance of sufficient loan-loss reserves by financial institutions;
(2) achievement of fair and transparent financial-sector administration by the Financial Supervisory Agency (FSA)[3] and strengthening of inspection and regulation based on prompt corrective action;
(3) promotion of restructuring by financial institutions to improve their operational soundness; and
(4) establishment of a process to deal with failures of financial institutions and the creation of a bridge bank system.

The administration sought the enactment of this proposed plan through a package of six bills presented to the "financial session" of the Diet, which followed the 1998 Upper House election. However, as I noted above, the negotiation process with the opposition led to the amendment of our proposals and the enactment of the Financial Revitalization Law and the Financial Function Early Strengthening Law.

The opposition proclaimed that the LDP had swallowed their demands whole by agreeing to the temporary nationalization ("special public management") of failed financial institutions, but in fact our original set of bills had included an arrangement for temporary nationalization through the acquisition of ordinary shares. Clearly, the plan that we had developed served as the foundation for the Financial Revitalization Law that was finally enacted in October 1998.

The two new laws served as the basis for dealing with the failures of the LTCB and Nippon Credit Bank and for injecting needed capital into the major banks, thereby allowing Japan to pull back from the precipice of financial disaster. We believe that these two Total Plans provided 80 percent of the necessary prescriptions for a revival of the Japanese economy.

Some progress has been achieved since then. For example, financial institutions have directly written off as much as ¥10 trillion in nonperforming assets over the past three years. At the same time, however, partly because of the application of stricter disclosure standards and also because of the further deterioration of the state of the economy, the volume of bad loans has increased. Moreover, financial institutions have not worked as diligently as they should have to deal with this problem.

Regrettably, we politicians were not sufficiently aware of the magnitude of the problem, partly because we did not have accurate figures available to us. Also regrettable is the fact that both the media and the general public have focused primarily on the handling of failed institutions and the infusions of public funds into banks, or they have been distracted by the showiness of the major alliances and mergers among banks and other institutions. This has caused them to lose sight of the root cause of the bad-loan problem.

The decision to inject public funds as capital into the major banks was inevitable. But even though the funds must ultimately be repaid, inasmuch as banks received this support from public funding, they should have taken fundamental action to resolve their bad-loan problems. They should also have taken the blame for allowing the situation to deteriorate to this extent, both by clarifying the responsibility of their executives and by drastically restructuring their operations.

At the time, the administration of Prime Minister Obuchi Keizō was placing top priority on achieving economic recovery through powerful measures to increase aggregate demand, including large-scale tax cuts and additional outlays for public works. On top of that, the government installed a safety net for small and medium-sized enterprises in the form of special public guarantees for lending up to a total of ¥20 trillion (which was later raised to ¥30 trillion). These measures, combined with the leeway provided by the injections of public funds, created favorable conditions for banks to resolve their bad-loan problems.

In fact, however, the banks failed to use this breathing period to deal resolutely with their bad loans. Instead, they took the easy route of writing off debts. And both the political leadership and the bureaucracy overlooked this failure. The bill for these two years or more of inaction is a big one. If the banks had proceeded diligently in dealing with the problem, we would not be facing the critical situation we are today.

The public funds injected for the purpose of rehabilitating the banking system had the perverse effect of magnifying the moral hazard in the financial sector and allowing efforts to deal with the problem to be put off, thereby accelerating the decline of the Japanese economy. This is a terribly unfortunate result, and we have now reached the point where further procrastination is impossible. We can no longer sit idly by and watch the situation deteriorate.

Survival Plan for the Japanese Economy

It was with this in mind that in spring 2001, as Prime Minister Mori Yoshirō and his cabinet were on the verge of stepping down, Ishihara and I, without any official support from the party and without knowing who the next prime minister would be, embarked on the task of drawing up a third set of proposals. We worked at a feverish pace to come up with a comprehensive strategy to clarify the state of bad loans, further increase the liquidity of land and credits, rehabilitate the financial system, revive industry, and put a stop to asset deflation. Below, I present a five-point outline of our proposal, which we titled the Survival Plan for the Japanese Economy: Breaking the Negative Chain of Events.

1. Strict Internal Risk Management and Reserve Funding

The market continues to be impeded by the lingering suspicion that banks do not have an accurate grasp of the financial condition of borrowers and are therefore classifying firms that are in danger of bankruptcy merely as "requiring attention." In order to alleviate this suspicion and restore market confidence, banks must implement a stricter classification of borrowers—paying special attention to the borrowers in the "requiring attention" category—and they must set aside reserves accordingly. In addition, strict external auditing by others must be sought, and the FSA must promptly conduct new inspections.

2. Removal of Bad Loans from Balance Sheets

As noted above, through stricter internal and external audits, banks must determine the extent of their loans to borrowers "requiring attention." Such loans should be removed from banks' balance sheets within a fixed period. The scope of the Servicer Law should be expanded to cover nonbank debt instruments, monetary claims that have been made liquid and securitized by special-purpose companies, and monetary claims of failed companies. Another measure that will facilitate this process is the strengthening of the functions of the Resolution and Collection Corporation (RCC), which has already contributed to resolving the bad-loan problem by buying approximately ¥4 trillion in bad loans from financial institutions and by collecting close to half this amount. Its functions should be strengthened and shifted along the lines of the U.S. Resolution Trust Corporation (RTC) in order to take better advantage of its human resources and expertise.

Finally, new rules are required for debt write-off that will assure social equity by preventing moral hazard and that will take into consideration whether the debtor corporation can truly be rehabilitated. The tax handling of such cases should be made clearer, and rehabilitation plans that may have adverse effects on entire industries should not be accepted.

3. Revitalization of Industry through Structural Reform

Efforts should be made to revitalize those industries (mainly in the nonmanufacturing sector) in which there are groups of companies that have excess liabilities. One means to do this is by expanding and increasing the use of legal provisions for corporate rehabilitation. Systems like those introduced in the newly enacted Civil Rehabilitation Law and Specified Credit Conciliation Law should be extensively publicized and actively applied, and the use of debtor-in-possession (DIP) financing should be promoted to provide necessary operating funds for companies in the process of being rehabilitated.

Similarly, the Industrial Revitalization Law for firms with excess liabilities should be expanded to encompass debt write-offs. A new set of standards for the designation of industries to be rehabilitated should be drawn up to promote the regrouping and streamlining of corporations where debt write-offs have taken place, including those in the nonmanufacturing sector.

Finally, with loan-loss accounting expected to be introduced in just a few years, the corporate rehabilitation procedures of the Civil Rehabilitation Law and the Industrial Revitalization Law should be actively used for companies still suffering the aftereffects of the bubble economy (such as firms in the distribution, real estate, and construction industries).

4. Increased Liquidity of Land Assets

We proposed a number of measures to promote the liquidity of land and credits in order to correct asset deflation and promote urban revitalization.

For example, instead of being allowed to remain frozen, bad loans and collateral real estate owned by financial institutions should be put on the market, and a "Survival Fund" should be created to set minimum prices for these assets. This fund—operating as a government-supported corporation—would securitize the assets that it acquired, thereby putting the market mechanism to work. By contributing to the development of the market for asset-backed securities, it would promote a fundamental resolution of the bad-loan problem. In addition, a real estate investment index should be created to assist investors in making accurate judgments, and the tax rates on real estate transactions, such as the real property acquisition tax and the registration and license tax, should be set at zero for a period of three years.

In order to promote urban revitalization, we proposed the creation of a new "Urban Revitalization Commission" that would promote such projects as a major expansion of Haneda Airport in Tokyo to transform it into an international, 24-hour facility, and the creation of a third major airport in the Tokyo metropolitan area through the reversion of Yokota Air Base from U.S. military use. The commission should serve as a catalyst for economic recovery by promoting concentrated investment in urban areas that promise to have significant economic ripple effects.

Also, the role of the Urban Development Corporation should be strengthened and its specialized expertise should be used to promote metropolitan revitalization, while the RCC, which lacks expertise in real estate, should enter into joint development arrangements with local government organs, private sector businesses, and the Urban Development Corporation in order to increase the value of its real estate holdings and promote their sale.

5. Supplementary Macroeconomic Policy Measures

Decisive action to achieve a final resolution of the bad-debt problem will inevitably have a negative impact on the economy, and so it is essential that this be countered with supplementary macroeconomic policy measures, including further monetary relaxation by the BOJ and employment policies that promote greater mobility. (The BOJ in fact decided on March 19—just before we completed our Survival Plan—to implement additional monetary relaxation, primarily through the reintroduction of its zero-interest-rate policy, pushing down overnight rates effectively to zero.)

Macroeconomic policy must also be applied in the area of employment policy to cope with the growth of joblessness that will occur during the process of structural reform, to promote the movement of labor into new fields, and to alleviate the mismatch between labor supply and demand. A comprehensive set of employment policies is required, including emergency job-creation measures, support for reemployment, the promotion of employment-creation measures centered on new and growth industries, the promotion of human resource development to enhance people's value in the labor market, the implementation of job-related education and training with a focus on unemployed middle-aged and older people, the promotion of job-sharing, and a limited extension of the period during which unemployment benefits are paid to soften the pain of restructuring.

Ishihara and I drafted this Survival Plan as a counterproposal to one that was agreed upon by the ruling coalition on March 9, 2001. We believed that the coalition's proposal failed to show a clear path to economic revival. In April, however, the government announced an emergency economic package that was drawn up on the basis of the ruling coalition's proposal. The specific content had been filled in by representatives of various ministries and agencies.

I am confident that our Survival Plan was far superior to this product of the bureaucracy-dominated government. The only way to achieve a proper resolution of the bad-loan problem and to revive the Japanese economy is to steadily shift these loans off financial institutions' balance sheets. As described briefly above, our Survival Plan proposed a number of such measures that would do just that, including expanding the scope of the Servicer Law and strengthening the functions of the RCC for adjusting and collecting nonperforming loans.

Concrete action has since progressed in some of these areas. For example, the Advanced Reform Program adopted by the government on September 21, 2001, did include measures to strengthen the functions of the RCC and a declaration of the government's intent to implement special inspections aimed at ensuring that financial institutions have the proper reserves for loans to borrowers that "require attention." And in keeping with our proposal that rules be established for debt write-offs, the Japanese Bankers Association and Keidanren (Japan Federation of Economic Organizations) set up a special group to study this issue and subsequently produced a set of guidelines.

Also, in September 2001, the Japanese stock market began trading in real estate investment trusts (REITs), funds modeled on U.S. real estate investment trusts, which will hopefully assist in dealing with bad loans. Against a backdrop of deteriorating investor optimism about the stock market, institutional investors looking for relatively high dividend yields have shown considerable interest in these new REITs, and it is expected that the market in securitized real estate (of which REITs form the core) will grow to around ¥10 trillion over the next ten years. There are also drastic measures under consideration at this time to lighten the tax burden on land transactions as a means of countering asset deflation, and the quantitative monetary relaxation undertaken by the BOJ should further help prop up demand.

Another urgent issue is the structural reform of the stock market. Here, it has been decided to reform the taxation of securities and to improve conditions so that more individual investors will be able to participate in the market.

Meanwhile, as noted above, the final resolution of bad loans and other measures that will have a strong negative impact on the economy must be accompanied by support from the macroeconomic policy side. In addition to the BOJ's monetary relaxation in April 2001, it took further steps in August and September to expand the scope of its quantitative relaxation and lowering the official discount rate.

While these steps are encouraging, the Survival Plan represents a much more comprehensive set of prescriptions for the final stage of dealing with the bad-loan problem. The path we have described is one that the Japanese economy absolutely must tread in order to revive. Unfortunately, since neither Ishihara nor I were in positions of responsibility at the time we drafted this plan, we were unable to achieve the same sort of influence as we had with our previous two Total Plans. Partly because it was drawn up to counter the emergency economic package put together by the ruling coalition, our plan was virtually ignored within the LDP. While our plan lacked influence within the party, however, we were able to have some impact on the discussions of the bad-loan issue through media appearances and interviews, and I believe that our discussions with bureaucrats as we were drafting our plan had some effect on their subsequent policymaking activities.

THE PROPER SHAPE OF POLICYMAKING AND THE ROLE OF POLITICIANS

Evaluating Policymaking under the Bureaucracy-Dominated System

As I have noted, the LDP held on to the reins of government and perpetuated the 1955 system for nearly four decades. Using the bureaucracy as their think tank, successive LDP administrations were able to turn Japan into the world's second-largest economic power. Although the bureaucrats were the ones who drafted the policies, however, it was initially a politically dominated system. Bureaucrats had superior skills and expertise with respect to policy drafting, but it was the politicians of the LDP who directed the bureaucrats and used the party's political strength to get the policies implemented. As long as the politicians understood their responsibility as the main actors of policy implementation, and as long as there was an appropriate degree of orderliness and tension in their relationship with the bureaucrats on whom they relied for policymaking assistance, this partnership functioned smoothly.

The Finance Ministry mandarins, who reigned at the peak of the bureaucratic structure, were deeply involved in the process of forming important policies and always provided input based on their own expertise. Sometimes they clearly went too far, as in the case of the proposal for a national welfare tax, which the MOF bureaucrats pushed the Hosokawa coalition government into accepting. However, those in the bureaucracy generally believed that they were supporting the country, and they included many highly capable individuals with a strong sense of mission. On the LDP side, meanwhile, there were strong figures who could meet the bureaucrats' expectations and make firm decisions when necessary.

During the 1990s, however, unexpected developments began to unfold as the economic bubble burst and the 1955 system collapsed. The relationship between the political leadership and the bureaucracy became distorted by an extreme degree of moral hazard. The most prominent example of this was the bad-loan problem. Even after the situation had deteriorated to the point where the mandarins of MOF were incapable of dealing with it by themselves, they still failed to take action. They justified their neglect by relying on overly optimistic forecasts for the economy, based on which they asserted that the bad loans could be handled once business took a turn for the better and land prices resumed their rise. Meanwhile, the politicians left the matter in the bureaucrats' hands, declaring financial affairs to be MOF's field of specialized responsibility. This combination of bureaucratic procrastination and political negligence resulted in a major delay in taking fundamental steps to address the problem.

The bad-debt problem also highlighted the limits of sectionalized bureaucratic administration. Since bureaucrats are bound by their ties to their own organization, they cannot take the lead in dealing with policy issues that cut across organizational lines among different ministries and agencies. This is where the need for a politically dominated system of policymaking becomes evident. And as I have argued here, our 1998 Comprehensive Plan for Financial Revitalization offers an example of one attempt to introduce just such an approach.

Japan is now at the point of its third great national opening, following the Meiji Restoration in the 19th century, which brought the country into the modern world, and the aftermath of World War II, which produced tremendous changes in the country's political, social, and economic systems. More than half a century has passed since the end of the war, and many of the arrangements that worked for decades are now suffering from systemic fatigue. We urgently need to carry out structural reforms and rebuild these systems.

Constructing a Politically Dominated System

Properly speaking, it is the role of politicians to come up with prescriptions for curing the country's ills and to offer direction for the country's future course in the form of concrete policies. Japan's bureaucrats are certainly talented, but it is simply impossible for them, however hard they might try, to match politicians when it comes to sensitivity to the voices of the public. The same can be said with respect to "footwork": the politician's job is to keep his or her constituents' interests always in mind and to regularly make the rounds to listen to the voices of those on the front lines.

What is important for politicians in the age of a politically dominated system is to develop the ability to formulate policies using their own minds. In order to seize the policy reins from the bureaucrats with respect to crucial policy matters, politicians need to study intensively in a way totally unlike anything the old-style, bureaucracy-dependent politicians did. And at the same time, politicians must have conceptual power, a sense of balance, and the power of persuasion. These are prerequisites for overcoming the old pattern of bureaucratic dominance and replacing it with a system in which elected politicians exercise leadership over the bureaucracy.

Under a system of parliamentary government such as Japan's, the proper shape of a politically dominated system is a cabinet-dominated system. It is particularly important for there to be a clear command center that can construct a national strategy and other key policies, and for this purpose, the functions of the *kantei*, the Prime Minister's Office, must be strengthened.

The reorganization of the central government ministries and agencies that was initiated by the Hashimoto administration was in part a response to this need. The new organizational framework that went into effect in January 2001 provides for a more powerful *kantei*. It has also sent numerous elected politicians into the ministries and agencies to hold the newly created posts of senior vice minister and parliamentary secretary. In this sense, the reforms represent a move toward a cabinet-dominated system.

Ironically, the cabinet in power at the time of this shift was one whose approach was quite the opposite of a cabinet-led government. Prime Minister Mori and his administration depended wholly on the LDP for the formulation of policy. As a result, contrary to the proclaimed strengthening of leadership by the cabinet, what we actually witnessed was an increased concentration of power in the hands of the chairman of the LDP Policy Research Council.

Unlike Mori, Prime Minister Koizumi Jun'ichirō has sought to wield leadership of a presidential nature, and his administration has taken full advantage of the strengthening of the *kantei*'s functions. The prime minister himself has taken the helm in such initiatives as reform of the fiscal structure, dealing with the bad-debt problem, and reforming the special public corporations (*tokushu hōjin*). Koizumi has all the qualities required of a political leader: zeal, spirit, and courage. But in order for him to be able to exercise his leadership even more powerfully, additional institutional support is required.

The existing support system provided by the chief cabinet secretary and deputy chief cabinet secretary is not adequate. We need to create a system that will provide direct support for the prime minister from a group of politicians familiar with the ins and outs of policy and that will make proper use of the bureaucracy. If a system is created that allows politicians to make full use of talented bureaucrats, the politicians will be able to accomplish a great deal more than what they could achieve on their own.

What I would like to propose is the creation of a formal national strategy team to strengthen the operations of the *kantei*. This would be made up of a small group of politicians well-versed in policymaking and good at following through. They would report directly to the prime minister and would be assisted by a group of specially selected bureaucrats from different ministries and agencies.

Prime Minister Koizumi has actively recruited talented people from the private sector to support him in his work. That is certainly one approach. However, such individuals do not have expertise at translating ideas into policy action. When it comes to making policies a reality, they are no match for politicians. In this respect, the situation is clearly different from that in the United States, where people from the private sector who are brought into the White House to serve as presidential advisors often are already familiar with policymaking mechanisms and have personal connections with politicians.

The job of fleshing out the structural reforms that the Koizumi administration is aiming to achieve should be handled by politicians with responsibility for policy implementation. This is the only framework that will enable us to create a comprehensive mechanism for a politically dominated system.

The Role of the Ruling Party and of Politicians

A politically dominated system requires parties—especially the ruling party—to have in place a policy infrastructure that supports their legislators. Under the 1955 system, the policymaking mechanism of the ruling party was structured logically. Within the LDP there were separate divisions, corresponding to the various ministries and agencies, that considered policy issues. The party's Policy Research Council reviewed the decisions of these divisions and sent those that they approved to the party's supreme decision-making organ, the General Council, for endorsement as formal party decisions. In addition, special committees were set up as required to deal with issues that cut across the organizational lines dividing ministries and agencies.

During the financial crisis of 1997–1998, the party set up a Headquarters on Stabilizing the Financial System, which was comprised of former prime ministers, and a special committee to promote the Comprehensive Plan for Financial Revitalization, which was a specially created panel of individuals who were selected without reference to the usual rules of seniority. Through these groups, the party was able to work in close coordination with the prime minister's staff in the *kantei*, thus facilitating a politically dominated approach that allowed Japan to ride out the crisis.

Currently, a similar approach is being applied to the issue of special public corporation reform—one of the Koizumi cabinet's top priorities—responsibility for which has been assigned to Ishihara, who is serving as minister of state for administrative reform and regulatory reform. The LDP's Administrative Reform Promotion Headquarters is also providing solid support for this effort.

However, the fact that the ruling party is governing in a coalition with two other parties means that the policymaking process involves adjustments among the coalition members, and this has inevitably brought changes to the traditional policymaking mechanism. Authority has become concentrated in the hands of the top policymaking officials of the three coalition parties, who together coordinate policy for the coalition as a whole. As a result, open debate within each individual party and especially the LDP tends to be stifled on certain matters.

Room for further study remains with respect to the proper shape of the policymaking process in a coalition government. But the trial-and-error experience of the past eight years shows the great importance of careful discussion during the policy-formation stage, transparent policymaking procedures, and efforts at deepening mutual understanding among parties within the coalition government. A major remaining issue is how to achieve an appropriate balance between party autonomy and agreement within the coalition.

Even if the political system is well designed, however, it will not function as it should unless individual politicians further develop their own capabilities. Politicians must of course study and improve their understanding of the issues if their policy proposals are to be of any practical use. In addition, in order for politicians to overcome the inevitable limits on their individual abilities, they must not simply rely on the bureaucracy, but rather they must develop the abilities of their own personal staff. Unfortunately, the present system makes this very difficult. Each legislator is allowed only a single government-paid policy staffer. In the U.S. Congress, by contrast, each legislator has an official staff of about 20 people. Of course, the U.S. legislative system is different from Japan's, so direct comparison is not appropriate. Even so, having just one policy staff person is obviously inadequate given the broad range of issues that legislators must address.

The problem is especially acute for members of the Lower House who are elected from single-seat constituencies, since they must deal with the entire range of policy issues themselves. Measures should be devised to provide them with their own "policy brains," perhaps through the creation of a joint staff shared by legislators or by strengthening the functions of party policy research bodies, which play the role of a think tank for a party's legislators.

Another issue that needs to be addressed is how to build a structure of coordination between the ruling party and the legislators who have been assigned posts in the various ministries and agencies as senior vice ministers and parliamentary secretaries. In order to strengthen the teamwork between the party and the government, it is essential to coordinate the particulars of policy. A liaison mechanism between the party and the legislators in the ministries and agencies could help accelerate the process of turning policy into action.

Finally, I should touch on the system of assigning posts within a ruling party. For example, the LDP's system for making appointments to key posts is based on a process of negotiations among the party's various factions, and the tendency is for posts to be assigned in line with seniority (defined by the number of times a legislator has been elected). As a result, the most qualified people do not necessarily get selected. In order to achieve a policy-centered system, it is essential that posts be assigned on the basis of qualifications. For this purpose, parties should create a mechanism that will allow individual members' aptitudes and abilities to be judged objectively. In this connection, the system used in the United Kingdom, which has a parliamentary cabinet structure much like Japan's, can be a useful reference: Legislators there follow one of two separate courses, namely, the path to a ministerial post or the path to posts within their party.

Thc Significancc of Member-Sponsored Legislation

In closing, I wish to touch on the issue of member-sponsored legislation. Under Japan's parliamentary system, and in contrast to the U.S. political system, the government (i.e., the cabinet) has the right to submit bills to the legislature. The link between the cabinet and the ruling party (or parties) is tight, even though it is not as strong as the bond seen in the United Kingdom. Under these circumstances, as long as the system of politically dominated policymaking is working properly—in other words, as long as ministers, senior vice ministers, and parliamentary secretaries are taking the initiative—it is acceptable for 80 percent of the bills submitted to the Diet to be sponsored by the cabinet. Even so, I believe that Diet member-sponsored legislation should be used more actively in the future as one way of diversifying the nation's policymaking tools.

Member-sponsored bills may be divided into three major categories. First is the category of full-fledged, thoroughly debated legislative proposals. Bills in this category deal with issues that the government cannot handle well. A good example of this is the Organ Transplant Law that was enacted in 1997. This member-sponsored bill dealt with the truly critical issue of whether brain death can be equated with the end of human life. The lively debate cut across party lines and involved the government and the general public as well as the members of the Diet. In the end, a law was enacted with provisions considerably stricter than those seen in other countries' legislation on this matter, allowing brain death to be treated as the end of life and respecting the will of those desiring to donate organs for transplant and those wishing to receive them.

The second category consists of bills aimed at accelerating the policymaking process on the basis of political initiative. These are bills submitted by legislators in cases where bureaucratic turf wars are likely to delay the bill-drafting process within the government. In my own experience, one such piece of legislation, the Law on Fixed-Term House Lease Rights, was enacted in two years, even though the expected time frame for drafting and passage as a cabinet-sponsored bill had been five years.

The final category consists of "issue-consciousness-raising" bills. These are bills sponsored by members who wish to point out the need for legislation on a particular issue. Opposition legislators frequently submit bills in this category. In many cases, the bills are offered as alternatives to the legislative proposals of the government and ruling parties. The contents vary greatly from bill to bill and the issues addressed are diverse, but it is rare for such bills to actually be enacted.

In addition to the above three categories, I have noticed some exceptional cases recently. In the ordinary Diet session for 2001, the bill on stock market reform, including the legalization of "treasury stock" (the reacquisition by a company of shares of its common stock, to be held in the company's treasury), which ordinarily should have been submitted by the cabinet, was handled as member-sponsored legislation. And the current extraordinary Diet session is expected to bring revision of the Child Welfare Law in the form of a member-sponsored bill.

Member-sponsored bills can be expected to become increasingly important in the period ahead in response to demands for greater speed in the implementation of policy. What will be most important in this connection is for politicians to have the will, talent, and conceptual power to draft new policies, and the powers of persuasion and leadership required to get their bills enacted.

NOTES

1. The "1955 system" refers to the long-prevailing system in Japan of having two major political parties, the LDP and the Japan Socialist Party. It took its name from the fact that both of these parties were founded in 1955. Under this system, the LDP held a solid majority in the national legislature, enabling it to maintain uninterrupted control of the government; the Liberal Democrats basically never even considered the possibility of losing power. The Socialists, meanwhile, were content to be the leading opposition party and displayed no ambition to grab the reins of government for themselves. But the split within the LDP in 1993 ended the age of one-party rule by the Liberal Democrats, resulting in the collapse of the 1955 system after 38 years.

2. In the new cabinet, formed just before the extraordinary Diet session, I was appointed parliamentary vice minister for health and welfare, and so I did not participate in the deliberations over the financial legislation during this session. As a person who had been deeply involved in putting together the Total Plans, I was particularly sorry that I was not able to take part in the final work of getting the relevant bills, including the provisions concerning the bridge bank scheme, passed into law.

3. The Financial Supervisory Agency (now the Financial Services Agency) was established in June 1998. Previously, the Ministry of Finance had sole responsibility for both fiscal affairs and financial regulation, but because of the problems resulting from this excessive concentration of power, it was decided to split the regulatory functions off and shift them to the FSA, which was established as an external organ affiliated with the Prime Minister's Office.

3

The Finance Diet of 1998

Furukawa Motohisa

As long as the so-called 1955 system of political domination by the Liberal Democratic Party (LDP) prevailed, the relationship of politicians and bureaucrats was characterized by the leadership of bureaucrats. Politicians concentrated on coordinating the vested interests of those parties affected by bureaucrat-drafted legislation. As the system became entrenched, certain politicians established vertical ties with officials in the various ministries and agencies, allowing the politicians to serve as representatives of the vested interests related to each organ of the bureaucracy. These politicians became known as *zoku giin* or special interest groupings of Diet members. Each ministry and agency associated with such groupings of politicians, whom the bureaucrats used to lobby for the protection and expansion of their own interests in the parliamentary arena. There thus developed a mutually advantageous system of give and take.

This way of organizing public affairs started to collapse around 1993. Until then, Japan's period of rapid expansion had seen the steady growth of the pie that was divided up among rival interests. The LDP then found itself having to rely on other parties to stay in power, and it became increasingly clear that a fundamental review of the political system was necessary.

Today, with no new modus vivendi in place between politicians and bureaucrats, the necessary policies are not being executed quickly enough. In this chapter, I look back at the events of the Finance Diet of 1998 that gave rise to talk of a new breed (*shinjinrui*) of policymakers, and consider both what conclusions might be drawn from the roles of politicians and bureaucrats and what outstanding issues emerge from a reading of their behavior at the time. On the basis of my analysis, I make recommendations for improving the relationship between the two branches of government.

PREVAILING CONDITIONS

The extraordinary Diet session held in the summer and fall of 1998 became known as the Finance Diet because the key issue was how to deal with the anxiety triggered by uncertainty over the outlook for the Long-Term Credit Bank of Japan (LTCB). This session was marked by an event unprecedented in Japanese parliamentary history: A bill submitted by the government was rejected, debate was relaunched on the basis of a bill drafted by the opposition (principally the Democratic Party of Japan [DPJ]), and the opposition-inspired bill was passed into law.

Three main factors influenced this unusual course of events. First, the ruling LDP had just suffered a major defeat in the House of Councillors election, held immediately before the Diet session opened, and had lost its majority in the upper chamber of the Diet. Emboldened by this result, three opposition groups—the DPJ, the Peace and Reform coalition in the House of Representatives (composed of the New Peace Party, now known as the New Kōmeitō, and the Reformers' Network Party), and the Liberal Party—formed a parliamentary alliance that was strong enough to prevent the government and LDP from passing any legislation, other than the budget, without their consent.

Second, this Diet session was convened at a time of economic crisis: Stock prices were at the lowest levels since the collapse of the bubble economy, and fears were being openly expressed that Japan's troubles would trigger a global depression. Hence, restoration of stability to the financial system was considered a matter of overriding importance and urgency. The government, under the late Obuchi Keizō, was the target of intense criticism at home and abroad and was even prepared to accept in their entirety opposition proposals if the proposals could thereby resolve the financial troubles and keep the government from being pushed out of office.

Third, some officials and media observers believed that the bill proposed by the opposition was better than the original government bill. More theoretically sound and practicable, slight modification would allow its stipulations to be carried out quite quickly.

Under the 1955 system, the main opposition party—the Japan Socialist Party (JSP)—had either flatly opposed bills proposed by the governing LDP or demanded partial modification, but had very seldom proposed full-scale alternative legislation of its own. However, the collapse of the 1955 system strengthened the view that opposition parties should be constructive and propose alternative bills. The DPJ in particular, being the largest opposition party, was and remains keen to demonstrate its ability to function as a governing party by putting maximum effort into preparing alternative legislation. As a result, it put forward a bill, related to the highly specialized field of financial policy, that was sufficiently complete and detailed for its precepts to be applied.

The changed circumstances also saw the emergence of the new breed of policymakers: young policy specialists who together thrashed out the issues and produced a revised bill that was eventually passed. The Finance Diet created a new image of politicians and prompted a reevaluation of the relationship between politicians and bureaucrats.

GOVERNMENT AND RULING PARTY ATTEMPTS TO DEAL WITH FINANCIAL PROBLEMS

Besides their basic socioeconomic role of accepting deposits and extending loans, financial institutions such as banks and securities houses had previously also facilitated economic growth by regulating the balance between savings and investment. After the economic bubble burst, however, these institutions stumbled under the weight of massive bad loans and, in November 1997, the bankruptcy of such big-name organizations as Sanyō Securities, Yamaichi Securities, and Hokkaido Takushoku Bank (HTB) effectively brought to an end the so-called convoy system of administrative regulations and guidance, by which the authorities had sought to keep institutions afloat.

A new approach was required to deal with failed organizations and dispel anxiety about the increasingly frail-looking financial system. The government's initial response came in the form of a pair of bills submitted to the ordinary Diet session in January 1998. The first was designed to reform the Deposit Insurance Law; the other was the Financial Function Early Strengthening Law. The bills were passed into law the following month. The measures included ¥30 trillion worth of public investment to aid financial institutions, comprising ¥17 trillion for the processing of failed institutions (¥7 trillion in government bond-funded subsidies, ¥10 trillion in government debt guarantees) and ¥13 trillion to shore up the surviving financial institutions' capital by such measures as underwriting their preference shares (¥3 trillion in government bond-funded subsidies, ¥10 trillion in government debt guarantees).

Prior to these bills, officials at the Ministry of Finance (MOF) considered it taboo to use public money to settle the affairs of failed institutions. This largely stemmed from the severe criticism the officials received for having proposed similar measures during the 1996 Diet session that had dealt with the failed housing loan corporations (*jūsen*). Although the shocking series of financial-sector bankruptcies in November 1997 blew away that taboo, there was a limit to how deeply involved the ministry could become in policymaking given the public criticism of MOF for various scandals, many relating to the lavish hospitality accepted by its officials from institutions they were supposed to be regulating.

The government's two bills had a number of serious flaws:

(1) They failed to provide a basic mechanism for processing bankruptcy procedures, such as a receivership system for failed financial institutions or a bridging bank to take care of their outstanding business. A large amount of public money was simply set aside for use in financial-sector bankruptcy processing.

(2) They left unclear the question of how to deal with failed institutions when no other organization could be found to take over their business, as was the case with the HTB.

(3) The capital injections they made available to healthy institutions failed to address the responsibility of management and shareholders, thereby encouraging the window-dressing of accounts.

(4) The standards and principles governing injections of public investment were left vague, as a result of which all key decisions were left to the Financial Crisis Management Committee (known as the Sazanami Committee after its chairperson, Meikai University Professor Sazanami Yōko).

So it was that in June 1998, just three months after Japan's major banks had been declared healthy and given injections of public money, the LTCB started to exhibit signs of serious financial weakness. Its share price collapsed, dragging down the shares of other banks, triggering a general stock market decline, and causing the value of the yen to fall on foreign exchange markets.

With the existing measures collapsing, the government and LDP drew up a new policy, the Comprehensive Plan for Financial Revitalization (the so-called Total Plan). This plan was produced by the Government-Ruling Party Conference to Promote the Comprehensive Plan for Financial Revitalization and included a bill to set up a bridging bank. However, the new policy was not designed to deal with the failure of a megabank like the LTCB but, rather, was directed at continuing the practice of finding merger partners for failed banks. The government, accordingly, sought to broker a merger between the LTCB and Sumitomo Trust & Banking. Hence, the six government bills relating to the Total Plan that were submitted to the Diet in early August did not include measures for dealing with megabank failure. At this point, the government still clung to the principle that major banks could not be allowed to fail.

THE DPJ'S RESPONSE TO THE FINANCIAL PROBLEMS

Those in charge of financial policy at the DPJ had realized quite early that the nation's financial problems were extremely serious and that a megabank failure was a real possibility in the near future. The perception became stronger still after the Yamaichi and HTB bankruptcies in November 1997. It was the view within the DPJ that the troubles which had brought Yamaichi and HTB down would eventually spread to megabanks. Accordingly, the party perceived an urgent need to establish a system for dealing with megabank failure that would prevent panic spreading throughout the financial sector even were one of the biggest banks to fail. The DPJ energetically pursued the issue in an attempt to find workable countermeasures and conducted hearings at which were expressed the opinions of academics and market players familiar with domestic and foreign financial affairs.

In the course of debate, two conflicting opinions emerged. Some in the DPJ felt that further handouts of public money to the banks should not be countenanced, while others felt there should be a bold application of public investment to properly and rapidly sort out the bad-loan problem. Gradually, those who saw the need for urgent measures using public investment were able to gain the understanding of the party. In the end, it was decided to use an approach that had been used in Sweden to deal with megabank failure: temporary nationalization. Although this was a most irregular procedure, it had the merit of being flexibly applicable to bank failures of any scale. Accordingly, in May 1998, the party began work on the drafting of a financial revitalization plan, including a policy for failed institutions incorporating the use of the temporary-nationalization concept. By the end of June, the DPJ Financial Phoenix Plan was unveiled.

Encouraged by the results of the July House of Councillors election, DPJ leader Kan Naoto instructed that the Phoenix Plan should be turned into a concrete parliamentary bill. Work on the project went ahead, with the assistance of the Legislative Bureau of the House of Representatives. The most contentious problem encountered in drafting the bill was the compulsory purchase of shares in failed banks. The Legislative Bureau opposed this position because of concern that it might be seen as infringing on Article 29 of the Constitution guaranteeing the right to private property. In the end, the provision was retained on the basis that it was for the courts rather than legislators to interpret the constitution.

Having made this political decision, the DPJ took the draft bill to the other opposition groups—the Peace and Reform coalition, and the Liberal Party—which had proposals of their own. By early September, a bill that included features of all three proposals had been hammered out. The resulting Bill Concerning Emergency Measures for the Revitalization of the Functions of the Financial System (Financial Revitalization Bill) was presented to the Diet as a joint opposition party bill.

PARLIAMENTARY DEBATE

The government and LDP flatly refused to accept that the LTCB was bankrupt and sought to ride out the crisis by merging the LTCB with Sumitomo Trust & Banking and injecting a large amount of public funds into the merged institution. The opposition parties argued that the artificial prolonging of the bankrupt LTCB's life, without any careful audit of assets and liabilities, would not eliminate the existing financial uncertainty. They called for a strict audit, a recognition of the bank's bankruptcy based thereon, and rule-based bankruptcy proceedings. While the two sides continued to argue over their positions, share prices continued to fall and the possibility of a global financial panic being triggered by Japan seemed increasingly plausible.

The deadlock was finally broken when DPJ leader Kan stated that he would not seek to make political capital out of the nation's financial problems, and Prime Minister Obuchi steeled himself to accept the opposition proposal in its entirety. The two leaders met and an agreement was reached on September 18. Work was promptly started on the bill's revision, based on the opposition draft, that entailed a series of working-level meetings between the LDP and DPJ, after which the negotiators would take the latest developments back to their respective party executives for approval. The initial meetings involved no bureaucrats, their role being limited to commenting on the draft bill brought back to the LDP executive from the meetings.

The relatively junior Diet members who participated in these working-level meetings became known as the new breed of policymakers—their discussions being very different from the horse-trading that had usually gone on at meetings between the parties' Diet affairs committees. The policymakers began with a theoretical discussion of the policy rules to be agreed upon, making it relatively easy for the frontline negotiators on both sides to establish a shared awareness of the issues; reaching agreement was then straightforward. However, since the upper echelon of the LDP still had some old-fashioned Diet members who did not understand this new kind of policymaking, time and again an DPJ-LDP agreement would be reached only to have an LDP executive send the draft back for further discussion. It took a lot of time and work to achieve a final agreement.

When the bill passed into law as the Law Concerning Emergency Measures for the Revitalization of the Functions of the Financial System (hereafter the Financial Revitalization Law), some within the LDP called for the creation of a scheme to deal with ailing financial institutions prior to bankruptcy. The LDP brought before the Diet another bill—the Financial Function Early Strengthening Bill (hereafter the Early Strengthening Bill). Both the Peace and Reform coalition and the Liberal Party, which had been in the DPJ camp for deliberations on the Financial Revitalization Law, aligned themselves with the LDP on this bill, which was consequently passed with only minor revisions.

A number of factors lay behind the change in political alignments. Ozawa Ichirō, leader of the Liberal Party, was keen to use the nation's financial problems as a weapon to bring down the Obuchi administration in a single blow, and was not pleased with Kan's declaration that he would not make political capital of the issue. Meanwhile, the LDP leadership was alarmed at the prospect of its younger legislators wandering dangerously close to the DPJ way of thinking during the working-level negotiations. So, while the young Turks were absorbed in negotiations on the Financial Revitalization Bill, the leadership reportedly was quietly applying the time-honored techniques of parliamentary deal-making to bring the Peace and Reform coalition and Liberals over to their side. In their zeal to pursue pure policymaking, the new breed of politicians exhibited some naiveté with respect to matters of political stagecraft. The situation mirrored a remark made by Miyazawa Kiichi regarding fellow former Prime Minister Takeshita Noboru: "Although reason seemed to be on my side, somehow things always seemed to go Takeshita's way." The Takeshita brand of realpolitik seems to have been at work with regard to the Early Strengthening Bill. In this case, the new breed of politicians grabbed the political initiative in the form of the Financial Revitalization Bill, only to have it snatched away from them in connection with the Early Strengthening Bill. In this respect, the Finance Diet cast in sharp relief the new and the old faces of Japanese politics.

REMAINING ISSUES

Diet deliberations on financial legislation require specialized knowledge. These deliberations are not as susceptible to the ideological solutions that tend to emerge from political debate and, in fact, have little connection with the usual issues of political debate. In the past, the drafting of this type of legislation has been left almost entirely to the bureaucrats. During the 1998 Finance Diet, however, politicians took the lead in lawmaking. The Diet session symbolized a shift from government led by bureaucrats to government led by politicians. In a sense, this is evidence of the extreme gravity of the situation in the financial sector: The situation had become a political issue. The shift to a government led by politicians also signaled an improvement in the quality of Japanese politicians, who were now capable of debating financial problems. But the shift also reflected Japanese people's loss of faith in bureaucrats who had made the financial sector their fiefdom while displaying a paucity of policy ideas and a propensity for corruption as revealed by numerous embarrassing scandals.

This is not to say that the Finance Diet was an ideal model of politician-led politics. Far from it. Rather, the Finance Diet served to demonstrate just how many problems needed to be overcome before a truly healthy system of politician-led politics could be established.

Market-Influenced Financial Problems

Due to market-driven considerations, the Finance Diet session ended with the governing and opposition parties coming to an agreement that satisfied neither side. Protracted discussions were pushing down share prices and, with all the talk about fears of a Japan-triggered global depression, it seemed apparent that the markets would not permit further political conflict.

The need to respond rapidly to market trends was one of the reasons that financial policy often had been relegated to bureaucrats. The democratic process of political debate and consensus formation is not suited to policy challenges in which daily—indeed hourly—fluctuations in market trends are a material factor.

Nevertheless, when financial policy entails saddling the general public with the burden of supporting private sector financial institutions, key political decisions must be based on a democratic process. The country's citizens are becoming increasingly less willing to trust civil servants to use the taxpayers' money as they see fit without some system of checks.

In order to resolve this apparent contradiction, a new division of labor between politicians and bureaucrats is required. When dealing with issues that demand a high level of specialized knowledge and a rapid policy response, a division of labor is needed that can generate policy which leads markets and is not merely led by them.

The Need for a Shared Perception

If policy discussions are to be productive, it is essential that participants have a shared perception of the existing state of affairs. In the case of the Finance Diet, there was a substantial perception gap among participants regarding the seriousness of the financial crisis confronting Japan.

Because those on the government side were not prepared to envision the collapse of such megabanks as the LTCB and Nippon Credit Bank (NCB), they had not considered procedures to deal with bank failures on that scale. Even LDP Diet members who could envision the possibility of megabank failures tended to hope that a solution to the LTCB problem could be negotiated by way of a merger with Sumitomo Trust & Banking, while the government's response to other failures could be framed after the Diet had passed a bill to set up a bridging bank. As a result, among the LDP Diet members there was relatively little sense of urgency. Moreover, the government stance was that, since a rapid disposal of bad loans could damage the economy, it would be better to deal with the problem gradually.

On the opposition side, some of the DPJ Diet members were conscious of the extreme danger posed by the financial uncertainty and of the destructive power of the markets that threatened to bring down one of Japan's megabanks at any time. The critical need for a safety net, to prevent panic from spreading even should the worst-case scenario come to pass, led to the proposal for a framework that would facilitate a bold, swift clean-up of financial institutions. Some of the DPJ Diet members were convinced of the need for the highly irregular procedure of temporary nationalization as a scheme to deal with a worst-case scenario. They also sought to compel banks to set aside greater reserves against losses stemming from bad loans and to undertake capital reductions and accept injections of public investment if they lacked sufficient capital. Their plan contemplated the transformation of the Japanese financial system in just two years.

The perception gap between the government and LDP on the one hand, and the opposition DJP on the other, gradually narrowed in the course of deliberations. As a result of compromise, in the final legislation no obligation was imposed on the banks to create reserves against losses, and the Early Strengthening Bill was passed with its provision for voluntary acceptance of capital injections. The DPJ's view was that if strict audits were carried out at all the banks and the banks were compelled to make reserves at a fixed rate against losses from bad loans, virtually all banks would be found insolvent or nearly so. The banks could then be dealt with under the provisions for dealing with failed institutions as specified in the Financial Revitalization Bill. The party saw no need, therefore, for the Early Strengthening Bill aimed at institutions not yet declared insolvent. However, in the course of revising the Financial Revitalization Bill, the compulsory measures disappeared. As a result, nearly all banks could be categorized as technically not yet insolvent and this created a need for the Early Strengthening Bill. This perception gap was the main reason that the DPJ had failed to adequately focus on the pre-insolvency processing of financial institutions, and was thus unable to muster an adequate response to the suddenly unveiled Early Strengthening Bill.

The complex and contradictory nature of the information available at the time was largely to blame for the difference in perceptions. Depending on one's source of information, one could have alternatively concluded that all the banks were absolutely solvent, that all of them were effectively bankrupt, or that their situation lay somewhere in between. On the Tokyo Stock Exchange, however, banking shares continued to sell in a manner reflecting the most pessimistic reading of the situation.

Even today it is impossible to state with confidence what might have constituted the most correct reading of information in 1998. It is no exaggeration to say that there were then no adequate standards for information disclosure, and that there was little available in terms of objective information. These days, how one goes about collecting and screening information in the process of forming political positions is a matter of great and growing importance. It is essential that we establish a system of information disclosure and supply that will enable politicians to make correct decisions on the basis of information that is as objective and accurate as possible.

Defects in the Policymaking Process

During the Financial Diet, the LDP's policymaking process differed from its usual approach, according to which bureaucrats would draft a bill, related LDP subcommittees would discuss it, and the party's Executive Council would then formally adopt it as party policy. This time, however, the draft for the Financial Revitalization Bill was drawn up not by bureaucrats, but by LDP Diet members in working-level consultations with opposition Diet members. The results of these consultations were then reviewed by the party's Policy Research Council executives and bureaucrats. Under the 1955 system, consultations between government and opposition parties had seldom focused on substantive policy issues, rather they had been exercises in gamesmanship in which each side struggled to lose as little face as possible. In that sense, the substantive cross-party discussions during the Finance Diet were a significant break with the past. Moreover, since bureaucrats were forbidden to engage in direct contact with opposition Diet members, they were unable to pull any strings backstage during the revision process—something that they were accustomed to doing even with bills submitted by Diet members.

The new approach led to confusion as the LDP attempted to establish its position, greatly slowing down the process of achieving consensus at the consultations since, as earlier mentioned, agreements reached at working-level talks were repeatedly overturned by the LDP leadership upon review by the party. This problem underlined the difference in organization between a bureaucratic institution and a political party, the latter lacking a clear-cut hierarchy.

In a bureaucracy there are general rules about what level and type of decision can be made at each level in the hierarchy. When a matter goes beyond an official's jurisdiction, he must consult his superiors before a decision can be made. Senior and junior officials work as a team, constantly exchanging information and coordinating views. This means that there is seldom any major difference of opinion between higher and lower levels in the hierarchy. Politicians, by contrast, tend to act according to their own agendas, and the relations of seniority and subordination are far less clearly defined than in a bureaucracy. Hence, it is unclear just what decision-making rights and responsibilities rest with those members of the Diet directly engaged in inter-party negotiating. On top of this, the very real differences of opinion among LDP Diet members involved with financial policy added further confusion to the decision-making process.

In the end, the LDP executive found it could not tolerate all the confusion over the consultations to revise the Financial Revitalization Bill, and resorted to old-style politics. A traditional backroom deal was cut to bring the Peace and Reform coalition and Liberals over to the LDP's side. The LDP Diet members who had been on the working team discussing the Financial Revitalization Bill with the DPJ were replaced on the new team that worked on the Early Strengthening Bill. This change of personnel was part of the reason for the basic difference in the thinking involved in the two bills.

Inadequate Opposition Strategy and Structure

The passing of a bill based on an opposition party's draft, in the highly specialized field of financial policy, after government-opposition consultations and in the form of a bill submitted by Diet members, was a turn of events entirely without precedent. This enabled opposition parties to demonstrate to the general public that, unlike opposition parties of the past, they had the ability to draft policies that could apply in the real world. It was also a sign that the DJP had the ability to draft legislation, and represented a first step toward a future change of administration. Even so, the manner in which the opposition went about proposing policy left a number of problems unresolved.

First, the policy compromises that were necessary for the opposition parties to form a united front resulted in some imperfections in the execution of the policy. The original DJP draft bill was governed by the principle that strict rules should be established and that accountability was necessary in order to stabilize the financial system in a stroke and within a short period of time. However, the need to present the draft bill as a joint bill by three opposition groups required some policy compromises. These compromises were necessary because without the joint opposition campaign, the Financial Revitalization Bill, with its radical provision for temporary nationalization remaining intact from the original DJP draft, would probably not have passed. Still, these compromises and others added in the course of government-opposition negotiations resulted in some problems in the application of the law.

A second problem centered around the issue of responsibility for the new law. Since the opposition was involved in drafting the legislation, it also had to bear a measure of responsibility for the way the law was implemented. In the case of the Financial Revitalization Law, a number of defects became apparent at the implementation stage, including the issue of who should bear the burden of secondary losses arising from the application of the law. Some of the defects increased the economic burden on the general public, leading to criticism of the opposition parties, especially the DPJ, as the original authors of the bill. The LDP and its governing coalition partners were especially vocal in condemning the DPJ on this point. However, it is the governing parties that have responsibility for running the administration and which should bear the blame for problems resulting from the legislation. After all, the government carries executive responsibility. If it finds defects in a new law, it should take measures to correct them. Instead of taking such measures, the LDP chose only to heap opprobrium on the DPJ as its original author—rather like a dangerous driver who causes an accident and blames the car.

A third problem involved the shortage of manpower. A total of six opposition Diet members, with only four or five assistants, drafted policy in the highly technical field of finance, worked out the fine details, and prepared the policy to become law. Apart from some technical assistance from the House of Representatives Legislative Bureau in drafting the bill, they received no outside help.

Absorbed in the Financial Revitalization Bill, and exhausted by the effort devoted to it, the DPJ Diet members and their staff were quite unprepared to deal with the sudden appearance of the Early Strengthening Bill. They did not have a chance to examine the bill until after it had been submitted by the LDP. With little time and a fracture in the opposition groups' united front, the DPJ did not have the energy to come up with an alternative blueprint that it could use to force the government to accept as the party had done with the Financial Revitalization Bill. The end result was that the Early Strengthening Bill was passed without having been subjected to sufficient debate.

The DPJ's frustration over this incident should be channeled into positive action. Stronger party machinery could improve the party's capacity to draft policy and turn it into legislation, preparing the party for the day it takes over the reins of government. To accomplish this goal, the staff of the party's Policy Research Council should be reinforced, and the party should build networks with outside specialists in every field who can provide assistance should an issue require special expertise. To this end, establishing the party's own think tank would be one possible option.

Antagonism between Politicians and Bureaucrats

Distrust of bureaucrats on the part of politicians led to the complete exclusion of the former from consultations between the government and opposition during the Finance Diet. Marking a clear break with an era when politicians relied on bureaucrats to think for them, the Finance Diet represetned a first step toward a new style of politics in which politicians would claim the leading role. The bureaucrats grumbled for some time about details of the legislation, which led to a rupture with politicians. Consequently, the bureaucrats declined to point out deficiencies in the legislation. It was these deficiencies that, once discovered during the implementation stage, placed an extra burden on the general public.

Because the politicians refused to trust the bureaucrats, they were obliged to check the legislation themselves—including the very technical details. Distracted by the fine print, the politicians failed to clearly articulate a clear expression of intention on the big-picture issues that really mattered, such as whether to aim for a hard or soft landing for the financial sector, and how soon to aim for stabilization of the financial system. All told, this was a classic instance of how the failure of politicians and bureaucrats to cooperate worked to the detriment of the nation. Since bureaucrats cannot be eliminated, politicians must make sure they are put to work in the public interest. Distrusting bureaucrats and so excluding their contributions to the policymaking process can hardly be described as responsible political leadership.

FUTURE RELATIONS BETWEEN POLITICIANS AND BUREAUCRATS

The age of bureaucrat-led politics is over. No longer will bureaucrats monopolize information and be involved in every phase of the policymaking process. However, even if it is recognized that the bureaucracy has lost its ability to wield executive power—to decide the future course and strategy of the nation, and realize that strategy through policymaking—and may not even be an appropriate agent to take on such a role, the fact remains that these functions are vital to the governance of the nation. Someone, or some group of individuals, must perform those functions if the country is to avoid the fate of an airplane that, with its pilot incapacitated, is heading for disaster with a cabin full of passengers. Whether politicians should take over the cockpit is open to debate. Clearly their role has grown in recent years, but given the present political system, there is a limit to how much of the executive function they can handle.

Regarding the issue of who should exercise executive power, it may be useful to consider two basic questions: What is democracy? What is the essence of democracy? As one model of state governance, few would deny that the objectives of democracy lie in the promotion of public welfare and socioeconomic development. It follows that a government, entrusted with safeguarding the livelihood, property, and rights of its people, has an obligation and responsibility to make decisions that are conducive to the well-being of the nation.

The essence of democracy that can meet these objectives is based on two key principles: (1) National (government) leaders are elected by the people and can be brought down by the will of the people; and (2) different ideas about how the rules governing issues should be decided lead to differing conclusions on the relative roles of politicians and bureaucrats.

While recognizing that both the above principles are present in democracy, the emphasis should be placed on the former, that is, on democracy as a set of rules determining how the authority to decide the will of the nation is generated. It is essential that the government should have the means and ability to decide an appropriate direction and strategy for the country, and to realize that strategy in the form of policy. While elections embody the democratic principle of majority rule, and politicians chosen through this process have democratic legitimacy, they do not guarantee that all the politicians have the ability and skill to run the government. Nor do democratic elections necessarily guarantee that each of the decisions made by politicians, through majority vote in parliament, will protect the livelihoods, property, and rights of the people, and be generally conducive to furthering the public interest.

Rather, the central role of the national parliament and its member politicians should be both to produce a government that can be entrusted with the livelihoods, property, and rights of the people, and to monitor the government and its legislative powers to ensure the government engages in self-regulation. It follows that if the government makes decisions that run contrary to the public interest, the parliament and its members can work through the medium of a democratic election to produce a new government.

Japan's bureaucrats, who are not at risk of being removed from their seat of authority by suffering electoral defeat, have not correctly fulfilled the role expected of them. On the contrary, their misuse of authority has led to a series of scandals that have blown away the old myth that Japan's well-being is assured by the excellence of its public servants.

Originally, public servants' positions were guaranteed so as to ensure their impartiality, since the main role of the administrative branch of government is to implement laws. Conversely, those who exercise executive power should not have their positions of authority guaranteed, since their role entails deciding the direction and strategy of the nation and turning abstract concepts into concrete policy.

The problems now confronting Japan would thus appear to stem from the failure of the cabinet to fulfill its executive function and adopt the correct organizational structure to fulfill its role. These failures have, indeed, left Japan appearing like a jumbo jet without a pilot. Hence the directionless drift of Japan through the aptly named "lost decade" of the 1990s. Japan urgently needs to break out of drift mode and progress in a clearly defined direction, to which end the cabinet must be reorganized so that it can properly use its executive powers. This was made abundantly clear by the case of the Finance Diet.

Japan urgently needs a cabinet that has democratic legitimacy along with a sufficient specialist knowledge to deal with academics and other experts. This cabinet needs to make decisions of principle and policy that are in the public interest. Under the current legal structure, the first requirement is that the ruling party (or parties) and the government be unified, as is the case in the United Kingdom. In the LDP governments to date, the government and ruling party have been spoken of as if unified, whereas in fact there has been a dual power structure—the government, particularly the cabinet wielding power, as well as the governing party (or parties), most often the LDP. The business of deciding policy has entailed parallel processes of coordinating opinion within the government and within the LDP. This has led to a blurring of the issue of responsibility between the two power centers, and the net result has been that both centers have been able to evade responsibility.

Once a party has been elected to office, it should unify its policymaking process with that of the cabinet. Party officials with policymaking duties—which, in the case of the LDP, means the head of the Policy Research Council and the chairs of its subcommittees—should be placed in the cabinet, and the ruling party's policy decision making must be focused on all the organs of government, especially the cabinet. This will make it clear that executive authority rests with the government, with the cabinet at its heart, and politicians will be able to proceed with drafting policy with a clear understanding of their powers and responsibilities.

In addition, adequate numbers of politically appointed staff members should be allocated to appropriate government positions. It is impossible to exercise control over the bureaucracy under the present staffing system, with each minister assisted only by a senior vice minister and a parliamentary secretary. It is necessary to increase the number of politically appointed staff members. It is important that these politically appointed staff members be able to work together under the direction of the cabinet team. Quite a large team would be needed, posing some logistical difficulty in bringing together all the members of the team after an administration comes to power and in making them work together as a team—even supposing one were able to draw them together. It follows that a political party aspiring to take office must form a team with its sights on the future before it actually comes to power. In particular, the party needs its own think tank to draft policy and foster policymaking talent.

Looking now at the internal workings of government, a clear division of labor needs to be established between bureaucrats and politicians (here meaning political appointees as well as elected politicians). Politicians should decide the basic policy principles and directions, after which they instruct bureaucrats to flesh out their proposals. Here it is important that politicians should have the ability to determine whether or not the detailed policies drafted by bureaucrats conform to the basic principles that they, the politicians, have specified. Politicians should also be responsible for explaining policy once it has been finalized. They should explain to the opposition parties, media, and public. Politicians must become responsible communicators, ensuring that people understand what the government is trying to do. Up until now, bureaucrats have fulfilled a large part of this function. In future, the U.K. approach, which bars bureaucrats from contact with politicians other than those who are members of the government, should, perhaps, be adopted in principle. The job of publicly explaining policy must lie with politicians who are in the government, and the job of bureaucrats should be defined as serving the politicians who govern. Once these roles have been clearly delineated, the key question of who bears responsibility for executing policy should also become clear.

As for politicians in the opposition, they are in a position where they do not and cannot take responsibility for the management of the incumbent administration. Naturally they should perform the role of scrutinizing and checking the activities of the cabinet, where the executive power lies. At the same time they should continue to work on and develop the policies they would want to put into practice were they to take over the government, refining them to the point where they are ready to be turned into concrete legislative proposals. As a part of this process, they should prepare for the creation of a team capable of controlling the bureaucrats—a team that could be pulled together and function smoothly as a unified entity. In preparing their policies, opposition politicians should not call upon the assistance of bureaucrats, and indeed they would not be able to do so were such contacts to be banned. Opposition parties would benefit from developing effective think tanks to take the place of bureaucrats in providing specialist advice. Opposition parties must develop the practice of gathering a wide variety of information from a range of sources and carefully screening it in their think tanks, with a view to formulating sound policies based on the relevant information. Were an opposition party able to develop its think tank to this level, it could tap the services of the think tank staff to support the cabinet when it to accedes to office.

Systematic support is required to create such an arrangement, particularly since maintaining and running think tanks entails substantial costs. For this reason, there should be some form of public funding provided to meet these costs. For example, an adjustment could be made to the system of allocating subsidies to parties in proportion to votes obtained at general elections or some of the funds now earmarked for the governing party could be transferred to opposition parties, on the condition that the extra funding be used for think-tank management. Since the governing party's access to the resources of the bureaucracy gives it a huge advantage over the opposition parties in drafting policy, it is only fair that some consideration be extended to opposition parties to offset the disparity.

The present Japanese political structure makes no allowance for changes in the administration and does not provide support to help opposition parties take over the reins of power. Moreover, even the LDP, which has been the party of government for so many years, has hardly any policymaking staff. Ultimately, this state of affairs has led to "the eternal administration of Kasumigaseki," a reference to the domination of politics by the bureaucratic district of Tokyo where most of the ministries and agencies are located. It is time that Japan shifted to a political system predicated on changes of administrations, as is the case in other developed countries. This would also help clarify the respective roles of politicians and bureaucrats.

Considering what form executive power might take in the future, one option would be a system of public elections for the post of prime minister. Directly elected by the people through due democratic process, such a prime minister would serve a fixed term and would form a government by staffing his cabinet with political appointments. This would bring to an end the dual power structure seen with the LDP and the government. The cabinet would formulate policy, which would then be debated in the Diet. The Diet, in turn, would monitor the cabinet's use of its executive powers and retain its present right to pass a vote of no confidence in the cabinet. Likewise, the prime minister would retain the right to dissolve the Diet.

Such a system would likely produce prime ministers with far longer terms of office and stronger authority over cabinet appointments than at present. This would result in greater self-awareness and a stronger sense of responsibility on the part of the cabinet in the use of its executive powers. The possibility of introducing direct elections for prime minister is currently a hot topic within the cabinet of Koizumi Jun'ichirō. When the pros and cons of such a system are considered, the fact that it would serve to clarify the character of the cabinet as the seat of executive power should not be overlooked.

CONCLUSION

The circumstances surrounding the Finance Diet left many unresolved questions as to the ideal form of politician-led politics. But it remains an indisputable fact that this was a breakthrough in the shift in the control of politics from bureaucrats to politicians, and it provided an opportunity for policy-minded politicians to emerge from the backrooms to center stage. Since then, there has been a rapid increase in the amount of energy and attention devoted to policy by politicians. There has also been an increase in the number of young people who want to engage in policy-driven politics and who are taking on the challenge of entering the political world. I am sure this trend will change the quality of Japanese politicians in the near future.

Members of the general public, too, hope that politicians will engage in more open policy debate. They are no longer satisfied with the old-style policy decision making in which politicians disappear into smoke-filled rooms to coordinate vested interests well out of the public eye, emerging only when deals have been finalized and they are ready to inform the public of their final conclusion. The public wants to see the issues aired, draft proposals published, have a sense of policy direction, and develop a clear understanding of the process by which those draft proposals are turned into formal policy. For the most part, politicians alone do not have the skills required to resolve the myriad conflicts of interest involved in issues with massive implications for the entire nation such as social security reform. Many of the issues confronting Japan today are extremely complicated and of gargantuan scale. The stage is being set for politicians with a flair for policymaking to get out in front and show the public what they can do.

Meanwhile, the world of bureaucrats is also at a watershed. In 1994, when I resigned from the Ministry of Finance in the sixth year of my own career in the bureaucracy, it was extremely rare for a young bureaucrat to abandon his profession. It is no longer so. Every year, more young people have been leaving the bureaucracy—some, like me, to go into politics, others to seek arenas of action in different fields. If this trend continues, Japan's bureaucracy will eventually be unable to maintain the caliber of professionalism that once led it to be called the finest civil service in the world. A lowering of the quality of public officials will be to the detriment of the public interest. Since we must have bureaucrats, they should be of the highest caliber, by which I do not simply mean individuals who are just good at passing exams but, rather, those who can respect the new relationship between bureaucrats and politicians, and can make that relationship work.

When these new-style politicians and bureaucrats come together to forge a new form of interaction—built on a new consciousness and according to new ground rules—we may at last be able to proclaim the birth of a true post-1955 system.

4

Information Technology: New Policy Issues and the Role of Politicians

Itō Tatsuya

On November 7, 2000, Yoshiki, a famous musician who was the leader of the popular rock band X Japan and who is currently living and working in Los Angeles, visited the then Ministry of International Trade and Industry (MITI) and met Minister Hiranuma Takeo, to whom he presented an opinion paper about Japan's IT (information technology) society. Yoshiki has a website that attracted more than 12 million visitors in its first month. He also created a video of a new U.S. band for Internet distribution, but in order for Japanese to view it, they need to have a connection 20 times faster than that of ordinary phone lines, and this sort of high-speed connection is not yet widely available in Japan. Yoshiki pointed to this type of gap between the United States and Japan and explained that he is painfully reminded of the backward state of Japan's information infrastructure every time he returns to Japan, which motivated him to submit his opinion paper to MITI.

The paper covered a variety of topics, including a call for the prompt achievement of high-speed Internet connectivity and measures to deal with the "digital divide." But one point that Yoshiki stressed was the issue of Nippon Telegraph and Telephone Corporation (NTT): "Unless the monopoly held by NTT is corrected, free competition will be impeded, user convenience will not improve, and the spread of the Internet will be hindered. At this rate, Japan's music industry will decline." In a conversation I held with him, Yoshiki noted that the sort of high-speed Internet service capable of dealing with the future advances in digital content, including music, is not yet well established in the United States. If Japan's private sector applied its energies and technology to that field, he declared, the country could create the world's most advanced Internet environment. Noting the need to adopt competition policy for this purpose, he urged Japan's younger politicians to use our power to make this happen. Yoshiki's opinions summed up the essence of the IT revolution, the limits of the policies adopted so far, and the issues to be addressed for the future.

As of November 2000, we were on the verge of the overhaul of central government ministries and agencies slated for January 2001, including the replacement of MITI by a new Ministry of Economy, Trade, and Industry, and I was effectively serving as MITI's last state secretary (parliamentary vice minister). In this post, I was strongly conscious of the transition to the new setup, under which the parliamentary vice ministers were to be replaced by senior vice ministers and parliamentary secretaries. The actual content of my work had been adjusted in advance in accordance with the new framework. Previously, the main responsibilities of parliamentary vice ministers had been the handling of behind-the-scenes parliamentary negotiations and attendance on behalf of the minister at various events and gatherings. But the new framework requires senior vice ministers to concentrate on answering questions raised in the National Diet. During the transition, in my capacity as parliamentary vice minister for MITI, I was involved in the full range of policy-related affairs, from the policy planning and drafting process to the formulation of proposed ministerial orders and the final decisions on important policy matters.

Through cooperation with other parliamentary vice ministers, we were able to deal with a number of policy matters that involved multiple bureaucratic organs, the resolution of which had previously been blocked by the interests of specific ministries. For example, the system of financing for business enterprises undergoing corporate rehabilitation (debtor-in-possession, or DIP, financing) that went into effect in fiscal 2001 (the year starting April 2001), and which is now drawing attention in connection with the rehabilitation of the major supermarket operator Mycal Corporation, was a product of solid and energetic teamwork between Shichijō Akira, secretary of state (parliamentary vice minister) at the Ministry of Finance, and me.

I devoted much of my time as MITI secretary of state to the area of information technology, a responsibility that Minister Hiranuma had assigned to me. With a sense of crisis at Japan's lagging position in the IT field, I worked to develop a clear overall picture, comprising new arrangements for costs, regulations, and systems, and played a direct part in the tasks of planning, drafting, and securing passage of the Basic Law on the Formation of an Advanced Information and Telecommunications Network Society and related legislation.

Since leaving my MITI post in January 2001, I have continued to be involved in IT-related policy matters, now from the side of the Liberal Democratic Party (LDP), serving as director of the Economy, Trade and Industry Division in the party's Policy Research Council and director-general of the party's Special Committee on e-Japan. Based on this experience, I would like to offer my thoughts—both from the perspective of the government and from that of the LDP—on the establishment of true political leadership and on the role that politicians can play with respect to IT, a policy issue that has major implications for every field.

THE IT POLICY RECORD

Rise and Fall of the Postwar Economic System

Building the Japanese-Style Economic System

In order to place in perspective the IT revolution, its policy impact, and Japan's policy responses, let us briefly review the history of the Japanese economy in recent decades. After World War II, Japan dynamically reformed its socioeconomic systems as heavy industry and processing and assembly activities took over the lead from light industry. In this way, the country was able to achieve international competitive strength and a position of comparative advantage in strategic industrial sectors.

Particularly from the rapid-growth years of the 1950s and 1960s through the 1980s, a major qualitative shift occurred in the economic system, which before the war had featured a flexible labor market, a capital market based mainly on direct finance, and a structure centering on *zaibatsu* (a handful of tightly organized conglomerates). By contrast, the postwar system came to feature a rigid labor market built on permanent employment, a capital market based mainly on indirect finance, a "main bank" system of close long-term ties between lenders and borrowers, and a structure of *keiretsu*, or relatively loose corporate groups. This set of arrangements was strongly supported by the bureaucracy-dominated policymaking system within the government. As a result, Japan developed a society with extremely limited mobility between organizations.

It was within this framework that the country achieved great success in raising the level of its manufacturing sector. The framework also demonstrated a high level of resilience in coping with drastic changes in the price structure, such as the oil shocks and sharp rises in the value of the yen. The weathering of such crises rounded out the success story of the Japanese economy and Japanese-style management system.

During this same period, trade friction between Japan and the United States greatly intensified. The United States demanded the dismantling of the economic system that was the basis for Japan's huge trade surpluses and its international competitive strength in cutting-edge industries. The Americans saw this system as being closed and anticompetitive, and they wanted the Japanese economy to open up.

U.S. Recovery and Japanese Collapse

Ironically, however, the 1990s brought a reversal in the economic positions of Japan and the United States. Japan's annual growth rate, which had averaged around 4 percent in the 1980s, plunged to 1.2 percent, while America's rate rose from 3.2 percent in the 1980s to 4.2 percent in the 1990s.

Japan's place in the international rankings of economic strength rose steadily through the 1980s, but this trend reversed itself in the 1990s. There was a widening U.S.-Japan gap as measured by a variety of indicators such as per capita gross domestic product, international competitiveness, and the level of IT infrastructure. Meanwhile, Japan found itself falling behind Europe and saw other Asian countries coming up rapidly from the rear and even overtaking it in the area of manufacturing.

Underlying this set of developments was the simultaneous deterioration of Japan's wealth-creation mechanism and of its income-distribution mechanism. Up until recently, Japan maintained its social stability by distributing the wealth earned by export industries to other sectors through the operation of *keiretsu* (with relatively strong companies sending profitable business to other firms in the same corporate group), official regulations (including measures to protect weaker industries), and fiscal policy (gathering revenues from prosperous industries and regions and spending them to aid the less prosperous). But the ability of export industries to rake in profits has been curtailed by the emergence of rival exporters in the developing world and by demands from major trading partners that Japan exercise restraint. On top of that, the rapid aging of the Japanese population has been increasing the domestic demand for intergenerational income redistribution. And to make matters worse, the lag in transforming the industrial structure through IT and regulatory reform has caused a weakening of the overall wealth-creation mechanism.

The result is a situation in which mechanisms for income distribution are excessively dependent on fiscal policy, causing tremendous budget deficits. As long as this system is maintained, those mechanisms are bound to collapse. We are thus faced with a critical dilemma: We cannot hope to maintain Japan's affluence unless we can manage to create a new system of wealth creation and an effective way of redistributing that wealth.

Dismantling and Rebuilding Network Industries

Regulatory Reform

Although Japan succeeded in reforming its industrial structure in the post-war years, it was unable to cope with the changes of the 1990s because of its failure to keep up with two major international currents. One was the current of regulatory reform in the network industries of the non-manufacturing sector. The second was the dramatic surge in IT. In countries other than Japan, these developments led to the breakup of traditional networks and the regeneration of new ones, a process that was accompanied by the erosion of existing structures of vested interests, the emergence of major new corporate players, and the passing of the baton to a new generation of business leaders.

From the 1980s on into the 1990s, there was a round of innovation in such industries as financial services, energy, telecommunications, and transportation, involving a fundamental shift of the standard from regulation of monopolies to discipline based on competition. In the field of energy, for example, the wave of reform started in the United Kingdom in 1990, with the introduction of wholesale pooling of electric power and the liberalization of retailing to large users of electricity. In telecommunications, the process started in the United States in 1978, with the court decision that allowed new entrants into long-distance telecommunication services.

In Japan, however, the process of regulatory reform constantly trailed that of Western countries, with steps being taken from several years to a decade later than in the West. This was because the bureaucratic establishment that had built up its authority through regulation was reluctant to lose the source of its own power. Furthermore, though it is important for the market to respond promptly to this sort of systemic reform, Japan lacked a culture of encouraging new entrants; the rigid labor market, the capital market based mainly on indirect finance, and the closed nature of the *keiretsu* groupings hindered reform and caused the process to lag.

Early Success with "Informatization" and Tardiness in IT

Another major change in the 1990s was the surge of innovation in information technology. If viewed in terms of the spread of the Internet, the lead is now held by North America, Nordic Europe, Singapore, Taiwan, Hong Kong, and South Korea. When it comes to broadband connections, South Korea holds a big lead, followed by North America. The United States, with its Silicon Valley, has become the innovation center for the IT industry, and places with close ties to it, such as Taiwan, India, Ireland, and Israel, have come to play key roles.

Meanwhile, countries like Japan, Germany, and France, which had constituted an advanced group second only to the United States during the period of rapid growth in manufacturing, are now trailing markedly. In other words, in the world of IT, earlier rankings of economic strength have completely ceased to apply and a new group of "advanced countries" has emerged.

In the earlier stage of "informatization" (i.e., computerization and information-network building) that preceded the IT revolution, Japan was seen as ranking number two after the United States. It was the only country other than the United States to develop a full-fledged domestic computer manufacturing industry. And it led in the automation and computerization of manufacturing operations, most notably in the field of machinery production. In that sense, Japan has experienced the sharpest drop in its position, from a star in the previous period of informatization to a laggard in the age of IT.

The Emergence of a Digital Information Market

The history of the information industry is one of separation by function and of battling with regulations and monopolies. The evolution of IT progressed from the narrow-band stage of reliance mainly on traditional phone lines to the broadband stage, where connections are independent of phone lines. And we are now shifting from a world in which three separate types of content—voice communications, broadcasting, and digital information—are supplied over their respective separate networks to a world where all types of information are produced, processed, circulated, and consumed using the same IT network.

The emergence of the Internet caused the process of unbundling, which started with the computer industry, to spread to the fields of telecommunications and broadcasting, leading to the rise of a market for the exchange of digital content encompassing phone services and broadcast programming. The rise of this market means major changes for industries using such services. Communication among limited groups of participants can now be replaced by the information market, and this is making it necessary to fundamentally change the way enterprises organize themselves and link up with each other.

From Economies of Scale to Network Externalities

The Internet is, both in its concept and design, something completely different from the phone network. The basis for the provision of cheap, universal Internet services has come from the linking up of different operators' networks in the context of competition among private sector businesses. The phone system, by contrast, was built on the basis of the economies of scale arising from market monopolies; high-quality voice communications were secured through the exclusive ownership of the lines linking users.

The existing phone system originally arose under a set of arrangements designed to regulate monopoly businesses as utilities and to protect users. The next stage was the opening up of the business to new entrants, a process that has continued through the present with the gradual addition of connection systems for essential facilities (i.e., equipment required in order to compete effectively). For the future, we require a major systemic and organizational shift from a framework premised on this sort of phone network to one premised on the Internet and on an age of convergence of telecommunications and broadcasting, a more flexible structure that will give the fullest possible rein to the energies of the private sector.

A key feature of the Internet is that, as seen in its technical standards (such as IPv6, the next-generation Internet protocol) and rules of use (for example, rules for domain names), the framework was first constructed not under government direction but through technical codes agreed upon by private sector parties, which have spread through the workings of the market. In terms of network infrastructure as well, the Internet grew through the voluntary participation of private operators making their networks conform to the technical specifications set within the private sector as they hooked up to the Internet. The operating principle here was that of "network externalities," referring to the fact that larger networks are more valuable to their users; this is quite unlike the case of the phone network, which was built to take advantage of economies of scale based on conformity with technical standards set by the government or by a government-sanctioned monopoly like Japan's NTT, which for decades operated as a public corporation.

For Japan, then, the most essential element of the systemic reform we now require is the maximum possible tapping of network externalities. And creating a competitive environment is an effective tool for this purpose.

The Essence of the IT Revolution

Information technology represents a wave of technological innovation that revolutionizes organizations and provides a new socioeconomic base in the form of the digital information market. In order to operate successfully on the international stage, companies must review their existing forms of organization, build new links with other companies through the information market, and redesign their approach to information openness, minimizing the scope of the core information that can be shared only within the organization. The "IT bubble" is said to have collapsed in the United States, but the share prices of American companies that have carried out organizational reforms using IT have held their value. In Japan's case as well, it is firms like these—the cohort of companies that have successfully reformed their organizations and that are advanced in their use of IT—that will be the source of new jobs and of the country's future comparative advantage.

REDESIGNING SYSTEMS AND FORMULATING A NATIONAL NETWORK STRATEGY

A New Telecommunications Law

How, then, should Japan redesign its systems to cope with the IT revolution? And what sort of framework can be created for a national network strategy for the future? The most important requirement at this point is to enact a new telecommunications law that will establish a system of full-fledged competition in the Internet field for the age of convergence of telecommunications and broadcasting.

Network businesses in the new age of communications and broadcasting must operate in an extremely complex competitive environment in which traditional telecommunications companies and broadcasting companies, phone companies and Internet companies, infrastructure providers and infrastructure users are all thrown together. Trying to tack on a new framework for the Internet and for the convergence of telecommunications and broadcasting in this context would be an extremely difficult process and is likely to entail endless efforts without resolution. It is not possible for a mixture of large and small businesses to set up the necessary infrastructure and to determine the rules for their use of the Internet under the existing Telecommunications Business Law and the Law Concerning Nippon Telegraph and Telephone Corporation, Etc. (NTT Law).

What is required is a new telecommunications law to encourage new entrants. The main thrust of this law should be to eliminate in principle all regulations not required for the purposes of securing fair competition and implementing antimonopoly policy. In concrete terms, I believe the new legislation should consist of the following four major planks.

Elimination of Business Segmentation

First, the new law should secure freedom to build networks flexibly. When businesses put together networks, they can do so either by creating their own infrastructure or by leasing the necessary parts of existing infrastructure from their owners. The present Telecommunications Business Law distinguishes between type I carriers and type II carriers on the basis of facility ownership; it does not allow companies the freedom to put together networks using whatever combination of owned and rented equipment that they wish.

Type I carriers are subject to a licensing requirement; type II carriers, however, are subject only to a notification requirement or to registration (if they use international lines). In addition, the 2001 ordinary session of the Diet adopted a separate entry requirement for "type 0" carriers (public utilities, government bodies, and other entities that own communications infrastructure but have no intention of providing communications services themselves, seeking only to rent out the infrastructure to network operators), classifying them as "carriers' carriers."

In order to encourage new entrants and promote competition, it is imperative that network service providers be able to design and build the most efficient possible networks by freely combining their own facilities with those owned by others.

Under the 1996 Telecommunications Act, the United States regulates only those businesses that provide services directly to the public for a fee; those that provide just conduits, dark fiber (i.e., the renting of unused core cables), or bandwidth are exempt from regulation under this law. The regulatory framework is designed with a view to securing appropriate services for users, and it does not concern itself with the sources from which network operators choose to procure the facilities or services they require. Japan should abandon its present system of segmentation according to facility ownership—a system not found in other countries around the world.

Even if the present segmentation is abolished, however, it will be necessary to retain a system of granting the required public utility privileges (subject to certain checks) to those operators who so desire when constructing their own network infrastructure. After segmentation is eliminated, in principle the requirement for all new entrants should be relaxed to one of notification. If the degree of freedom of infrastructure use were thus increased, competition would be promoted, and user fees and network service costs could be expected to fall; this would enable Japan to escape its present environment of network service costs, which are considered high by global standards.

Expansion of the Scope of Connection Rules

The second major plank of the new law should be the expansion of the scope of connection rules. The present Telecommunications Business Law does not provide an adequate framework for cases where new entrants are seeking to use the networks of NTT East and NTT West, the two regional subsidiaries of NTT that operate the local phone networks. All the law guarantees is access to local and long-distance exchanges. In order to provide additional network services, a broader range of connection rules is required. Also, to enable new entrants to expand their services, access should be guaranteed at every point where it is technically possible.

There is a particularly urgent need to establish a system of new connection rules for subscription-based metal cable and fiber-optic cable networks. The new connection rules should also include so-called collocation rules to allow competitors to install equipment other than exchanges, such as DSL modems and optical communication devices, within NTT facilities.

Establishment of Rights-of-Way for Cable Installation

The third plank of the new law should be the establishment of rights-of-way for cable installation.* New providers of network services who install their own cables, such as fiber-optic cables or coaxial TV cables, can either (a) lay the cables entirely on their own or (b) install them using

* Rights-of-way refers to the physical premises or facilities of a third party used by telecommunications and cable television companies to deliver services to their customers. Rights-of-way allows companies to install and maintain the equipment necessary to supply their services.

existing utility poles or conduits. President Son Masayoshi of Softbank Corp. has declared that if existing infrastructure like utility poles were made available, the resulting competition would generate a significant amount of demand.

In case (a), which applies mainly to new network operators providing services for offices, the operator lays its own cable all the way to the user, usually underground. In Japan, foreign-affiliated businesses in particular tend to choose this approach. However, this option entails numerous problems; there has been strong criticism, for example, of the high cost of excavation in comparison to other countries and the excessively time-consuming process. These issues of bureaucratic procedures need to be addressed as part of a thorough overhaul of the present regulatory framework, which should include the implementation of "one-stop service" rather than the multiple procedures now in place concerning rights-of-way involving national and local government authorities.

Case (b) is when the new network operator installs cables for ordinary households and offices by renting the use of existing infrastructure—utility poles, underground conduits, multipurpose underground ducts, and manholes—from the owners, such as NTT and electric power companies. The rules for cable installation of this sort are determined by private contracts, and the Telecommunications Business Law does not guarantee rights-of-way. In order to improve this situation, I think that a set of guidelines should be provided concerning what is considered acceptable and unacceptable behavior from the standpoint of the Antimonopoly Law, thereby promoting discipline among public utilities. There should also be provisions for dispute settlement in line with these guidelines.

Expanded Use of Radio Waves

The fourth plank of the new law should be the expansion of use of the radio wave spectrum. In recent years, the explosive growth of Internet use, technological advances, and the acceleration of transmission speeds have led to the rapid growth of demand for network services for a variety of uses in the area of wireless communication as well. In Japan, frequencies are assigned basically by type of service, and those services of a highly public nature have ample frequency bands. Frequencies have also been assigned to private sector services, but the bandwidth for business use is not adequate, thereby hindering the full-fledged implementation of new wireless services.

For example, i-mode, a service that allows mobile phone users to connect to the Internet, has been a big hit, but it can only be used on mobile handsets; the limitations of the bandwidth available for mobile phone transmissions keep it from serving as a medium for high-speed computer networking. SpeedNet Inc., a company set up by Softbank, Tokyo Electric Power Company, and Microsoft, was planning to launch a flat-rate wireless Internet service for home users in 2001 using the 5 gigahertz (GHz) frequency band, but it faces the prospect of having to limit this service because of the severe conditions required to prevent interference with the meteorological radar that is already using the frequencies in the 5.25–5.35 GHz band.

Aggravating this situation is the fact that, despite declining use of certain bands that have already been assigned, those assignments are fixed, and it is not possible to reassign underutilized frequencies for new uses. This amounts to a restraint of competition. In order to allow the growth of new wireless services for the Internet and other networks, we must reopen the frequency assignments in such underutilized bands.

As a first step, the administrative system for radio waves must be made more transparent. The only data currently released involves items like the existing assignments of frequencies to wireless stations by type of service and the assigned frequency bands categorized by general type of use. It is virtually impossible to determine from this information how effectively the radio waves are actually being used. Now that the Law Concerning the Disclosure of Information that Administrative Organs Hold (the so-called Freedom of Information Act) has gone into effect and government organs are actively working to provide freer access to the information they hold, it would be appropriate to release all the data indicating the actual current use of frequency bands. If this information were made widely available and it became clear which frequencies were currently unused or underused, then people could start concrete discussions about reassigning bands and reconsidering how radio waves should be used.

Since the opening up of radio wave bands is an issue of open access to essential facilities, we need to establish a system that will assure fairness. For example, there needs to be a set of guidelines to serve as cross-sector rules under the Antimonopoly Law, just as with respect to the issue of rights-of-way for cable installation. And at the same time, as we strive for greater transparency in the public administration of radio waves, I believe we should designate special bands where frequencies are going unused or where the market value of the frequencies is rapidly declining as special bands that would be made available for general-use network services.

Reforming the Structure of NTT

Reform of the structure of NTT is also an important issue in the context of creating a national network strategy. I believe that the restructuring of the NTT Group, by eliminating the problems of monopolization and securing the operational autonomy of the individual companies in the group, can promote the healthy growth of the network market. In order to achieve the desired results, we need to consider separately NTT's "universal service" operations (i.e., its public utility side) and its other operations (its private business side).

The government is responsible for establishing the necessary public utility arrangements and conducting regulatory oversight with respect to fixed-line phone service, which is an essential service for the general public. This service should be handled by the NTT parent company and the two regional operating subsidiaries, NTT East and NTT West. The group's other IT-related operations should be handled by separate, private companies, namely, NTT DoCoMo, NTT Communications, and NTT Data. To the extent that these private companies are dominant in their respective markets, they should naturally be required to avoid monopolistic practices and follow the competitive rules of the Antimonopoly Law.

One question here is how far the scope of "universal service" should extend with respect to network services, and how the providers of such services should be set up. I personally believe that the scope of universal service, which is provided by allowing monopoly arrangements that go against market principles, should be limited to fixed-line phone service, which can be regarded as a necessity for people's lives. Otherwise, we will continue to have a mixture of the mutually contradictory approaches of expansion of service through market mechanisms and of a monopoly situation. The idea of extending the scope of universal service to include mobile phones should be left for future consideration.

As to the issue of service providers, for the immediate future these should be limited to NTT East and NTT West, which are effectively now providing local phone services on a monopoly basis. I believe that these companies should be required, as at present, to provide universal service and that their rates should be subject to official discipline. Even if the present NTT Law is repealed, these points should be provided for under other legislation.

Another important matter that must be considered is the issue of national sovereignty in the area of telecommunications. The only remaining restraint on foreign investment in the telecommunications business is the 20 percent limit on foreign ownership of the NTT holding company. There is also a provision under the NTT Law that the government is to hold at least one-third of the shares of this company, so that even if the 20 percent limit were eliminated, it is extremely likely that the government would continue to be the largest shareholder and thus would still be able to exercise management control.

Some suggest that the present limits on foreign ownership of NTT shares should be revised. My opinion is that it would be appropriate to do so in order to facilitate the formation of international alliances through exchanges of shares and similar arrangements. And it would be desirable for the government to divest itself of all its remaining shares in NTT at an appropriate juncture in the near future so as to secure independence for the company's management and to allow the government to pay off some of its massive debts.

Inasmuch as the government is responsible for regulating the provision of universal service to the general public by NTT East and NTT West, we should exercise caution in checking the conformity to public-service requirements in the case of the direct operation of fixed-line phone services by foreign-owned entities. By way of reference, the United States has the means to assure national security with respect to foreign investment in its telecommunications sector both under the provisions of the Defense Production Act and under the review process applied by government regulators.

Competition Policy and the Regulatory System

The final issue is that of establishing a neutral regulatory agency and dispute-settlement organ to ensure that competition policy is properly implemented. This subject has been deliberated by the IT Strategy Council, and Japan has also received a warning from the European Union that it may lodge a complaint with the World Trade Organization unless the Japanese government pledges to establish an independent regulatory organ for the telecommunications market (*Financial Times* 9 November 2000). This was also at the top of the list of requests made by the United States in the Japan-U.S. talks on deregulation. The reorganization of central government organs implemented in January 2001 did not separate the functions of promotion, policy evaluation, and regulatory oversight. As a top-priority issue of administrative reform, we need to promptly separate these functions through such measures as the establishment of a neutral regulatory organ comparable to America's Federal Communications Commission.

Above, I have expressed my views concerning network strategy from the perspectives of cost, rules, and systems. The IT revolution will continue to progress rapidly even without government investment in public works infrastructure, provided we establish rules that will promote fair competition and allow demand to emerge. We must not forget that the countries that have succeeded in developing their networks are those that have halted government intervention, rejected the indiscriminate use of public funds, and firmly implemented competition policies. We need to move with utmost speed to create a system-design strategy based on a clear view of the future and the perspective of the users.

In addition, what we need for the period ahead is the implementation of a comprehensive set of policies. Merely modifying the existing policies one by one will not enable us to move forward with the desired IT reform. The policies for the various fields I have been discussing cannot be mere linear extensions of existing approaches; we must recognize the limitations of our earlier policies and abandon our traditional approach, starting over with a redesigned set of policies and systems. This is why the IT field requires a new policymaking process that is based on political initiative and that transcends bureaucratic sectionalism.

CHANGES IN THE IT POLICYMAKING PROCESS

The IT Strategy Council and Basic IT Strategy

The government sought to respond to this situation and to make IT a pillar of the Japanese economy with the establishment in July 2000 of an IT Strategy Headquarters, consisting of the cabinet members responsible for IT-related areas. The prime minister assumed the post of headquarters chief, and the minister in charge of IT, the minister of international trade and industry, and the minister of posts and telecommunications were appointed deputy chiefs. In addition to this group within the cabinet, the government set up an IT Strategy Council, consisting of expert members, to develop strategy proposals.

The IT Strategy Council met six times, starting on July 18, and on November 27 it came out with a Basic IT Strategy, aimed at turning Japan into the world's most advanced IT nation within five years. The focus of this strategy was on building an ultra-high-speed Internet network and improving competition policy; promoting electronic commerce; making a reality of electronic government; and fostering high-quality human resources for the new era.

Under the leadership of Sakaiya Taichi, minister in charge of IT, and with Sony Corp. Chairman Idei Nobuyuki as its chairman, the IT Strategy Council was thus able in the space of five months to come up with a basic overall strategy blueprint, based on a process of deliberation in which the private sector council members constantly took the lead. However, the private sector membership included representatives of firms in the IT business, and unfortunately the group proved unable to propose an adequate set of concrete measures in the areas of structural reform of NTT (a major client for some of their firms) or competition policy. Herein we see the limitations of private sector initiative in policymaking. In an area like IT, where a major change of policy direction is required, the need became apparent for a new arrangement to allow forceful policymaking, adding together the momentum for reform among politicians and that within the private sector. Based on this recognition among the politicians responsible for IT policy, a Special Committee on e-Japan was set up within the LDP, as I will describe below.

The IT Strategic Headquarters and the e-Japan Priority Policy Program

On January 22, 2001, the government set up a new IT Strategic Headquarters, composed of ministers from the IT Strategy Headquarters and private citizens from the IT Strategy Council. The new body took the Basic IT Strategy as proposed by the IT Strategy Council in November 2000 as its starting point and decided on a number of additional specific objectives, including: (a) the creation of an environment to provide 24-hour connection to high-speed Internet access networks at affordable rates for at least 30 million households and to ultra-high-speed Internet access networks for 10 million households within five years; (b) the promotion of economic structural reforms and the strengthening of the international competitiveness of industry through the use of IT, enabling sustained economic growth and job creation; (c) the achievement of e-government (the on-line networking of ministries and agencies) by fiscal 2003; (d) the achievement of growth in e-commerce, aimed at achieving a market scale well above ¥70 trillion by 2003; and (e) the surpassing of the United States' standard of human resources in terms of IT technical experts and researchers and the creation of an environment for constant research and development. The IT Strategic Headquarters then put together an e-Japan Priority Policy Program to give concrete shape to the government's e-Japan Strategy under Article 35 of the Basic Law on the Formation of an Advanced Information and Telecommunications Network Society.

In the course of drawing up the concrete policies, however, the strategic direction became increasingly vague. The related bureaucratic organs started to put up resistance. First of all, in the selection of members for the IT Strategic Headquarters, the private sector experts who had strongly argued for the inclusion of competition policy measures were left out. And in the drafting of the priority policy program, in comparison with the original Basic IT Strategy, greater weight was placed on the adjustment of interests among the relevant ministries and agencies; the result was thus a something-for-everyone set of policies that gave priority to measures put forward at the initiative of bureaucrats representing their own organizations.

The LDP's Special Committee on e-Japan

In connection with the government's drafting of the e-Japan Priority Policy Program, the LDP set up its own Special Committee on e-Japan headed by Kamei Yoshiyuki, then acting chairman of the party's Policy Research Council, to distill ideas from within the party and work for their inclusion in the government's program. Subsequently, following the launch of the administration of Prime Minister Koizumi Jun'ichirō, the chairmanship of the Special Committee went to Asō Tarō, the party's new Policy Research Council chair, who had previously served as minister in charge of IT. Responsibility for the secretariat was assigned to the council's directors of the Cabinet Division, the Public Management, Home Affairs, Posts and Telecommunications Division, and the Economy, Trade and Industry Division. The organization of the committee was beefed up to include all the relevant Policy Research Council officers and division directors. This was a product of the clear recognition by the Special Committee's previous chairman that it would not be possible to move ahead with a forceful set of IT policies unless the sectionalism of the bureaucracy could be overcome through LDP initiative. A new form of politics-dominated policymaking thus took shape in the IT field, with the LDP providing support for the cabinet.

Elimination of Duplicate Appropriations

The first task that the Special Committee undertook was the elimination of duplicate appropriations and the optimization of the IT-related budget. The total IT-related budget for fiscal 2001, including special account items, came to about ¥1.9 trillion. The committee examined this budget in detail, checking every project costing ¥1 billion or more. The key questions examined were the following: Is there duplication among budget appropriations due to uncoordinated budget requests from different ministries or from different bureaus or divisions within the same agency in such fields as electronic government and the promotion of IT at the regional level? Have the opinions of users been adequately reflected in the design of IT promotion policies? Have systems been designed to work in tandem with the related systems of other ministries, agencies, and local government bodies, and has interoperability been secured? Have the details of the contracts for the systems been made public? Will the implementation of the appropriations in question contribute to greater user convenience, lessening of burdens, and the optimization and enhancement of administrative operations? And if so, how can these benefits be expressed in quantitative terms?

Based on this process, the Special Committee came up with a concrete set of rules for the thorough elimination of duplicate appropriations: (1) appropriations that may duplicate others are to be clarified and consolidated; (2) new systems are to be designed not on the basis of totally new basic specifications but making effective use of the general-purpose systems already developed by the Ministry of Economy, Trade and Industry (METI) and the Ministry of Land, Infrastructure and Transport, the two leading ministries in system development; (3) specifications are not to be such that only a particular vendor can provide the required services; (4) in cases where users' opinions have not been adequately reflected, measures are to be taken to correct this; (5) systems that are not interoperable are to be made so except where special circumstances make this impossible; (6) if orders are placed by discretionary contracts, the contents are to be made public, and as much as possible, the use of such contracts is to be replaced by the open tender system; (7) through the disclosure of contract contents, a database is to be created that will provide standards for setting appropriate prices.

In this way, the party created a framework that made it possible to stop the mechanical apportioning of the IT budget among the relevant ministries and agencies and to instead produce a strategically prioritized set of appropriations based on coordination among the various bureaucratic organs.

Up until now, the process of checking requests for appropriations, which is the job of the Budget Bureau in the Ministry of Finance, has been handled by bureaucrats assigned responsibility for specific ministries or agencies. In other words, the process has been sectionalized. This has placed limits on the bureau's ability to assess requests across sectional lines. The Special Committee addressed this shortcoming by carrying out a meaningful, across-the-board check, based on which it was able to offer specific recommendations for making optimal use of the available funds. For example, it was able to propose the elimination of duplication in the work of developing systems for on-line administrative processing in different organs and to suggest using the money thus saved for the development of on-line procurement and tax-collection systems. Similarly, it was able to propose the consolidation of appropriations for the promotion of IT at the regional level and suggest using the savings to provide increased security for the IT market and to implement the e!Project, which aims to inform the general public about the fruits of the IT revolution. What made it possible for the Special Committee to offer these concrete recommendations was the involvement of the Policy Research Council division directors, who are familiar with the details of the budgets for the individual bureaucratic organs.

Advanced Implementation of e-Government

One of the targets under the e-Japan Priority Policy Program was to implement electronic government, or e-government, by fiscal 2003. But in view of the bleakness of the current economic situation, the Special Committee devoted its energy to getting the schedule for the related projects and procedures moved up as far as possible, seeing e-government as a source of IT-related demand from the public sector.

As a result of these efforts, the IT Strategic Headquarters adopted a clear policy of early implementation of e-government, and Katayama Toranosuke, minister of public management, home affairs, posts and telecommunications, announced that the target rate of completion for on-line networking of ministries and agencies by the end of fiscal 2002 would be hiked from 35 percent to 50 percent. In addition, the Special Committee pushed for maximally front-loaded implementation, with a call for specific measures to implement additional moves on the part of those ministries and agencies whose fiscal 2002 rate of completion falls below 20 percent.

As in its drive to eliminate duplicate appropriations and optimize the IT-related budget, the Special Committee issued concrete measures to be taken and published the results. Also, the Special Committee sought to achieve streamlining and rationalization of administrative operations and to reduce the burden on corporations through the prompt implementation of systems of oversight and of electronic bid submission and bid opening systems for the government's public-works and non-public-works procurement. It called for the study of a system that would specifically reflect the fruits of this form of computerization in the budget. As a result, the liaison council on the promotion of CALS/EC (continuous acquisition and life-cycle support/electronic commerce) in public works, headquartered in the Ministry of Land, Infrastructure and Transport, and the liaison council on the promotion of on-line government procurement, headquartered in the Cabinet Secretariat, worked together and reported the concrete results of their studies to the Special Committee.

The committee also made recommendations concerning electronic local government. First, in order to avoid the inefficiency of separate development efforts by individual local government bodies and to place priority on users' convenience, they recommended that the focus be on building general-purpose systems. Except where there are special circumstances, existing systems should be used, and they should be integrated and standardized to secure compatibility and interoperability. Second, in order to construct electronic local government efficiently and fairly, the committee recommended that all local government IT contracts, including breakdowns of the amounts to be paid, should be made public. Third, in order to provide incentives for local electronic government, support should be given to local government bodies that are progressive in implementing e-government, and concrete measures should be considered to reward those local governments that undertake this process promptly.

Finally, in order to secure effective responses to the above recommendations, the Special Committee directed the interagency liaison council on promotion of on-line local government operations, based in the Cabinet Secretariat, to compile and make public the concrete results of these efforts.

Making Government Fiber-Optic Cables Available

The Special Committee's close check of the IT-related budget revealed great unevenness in the installation of fiber-optic cables. For example, the Ministry of Land, Infrastructure and Transport has been moving ahead with installation of such cables separately along roads, rivers, and sewage lines without having made clear any overall plan. Meanwhile, the Ministry of Agriculture, Forestry and Fisheries and the Ministry of Public

Management, Home Affairs, Posts and Telecommunications have also been installing fiber-optic cables to promote the development of farming communities and local regions. But it became clear that no organ was bringing together all these plans to coordinate the installation of fiber-optic cables nationwide.

The Special Committee accordingly had information urgently compiled and made public concerning the current state of installation of fiber-optic cables owned by the national government and local government bodies and of those belonging to private sector organizations, such as telecommunications companies, electric power companies, and railway companies; a preliminary report was issued based on this information. This led to a decision by the government's IT Strategic Headquarters on September 14, 2001, to make the national government's fiber-optic network available for low-cost leasing by private sector telecommunications companies by the end of that fiscal year.

The Special Committee also called on the national government and local government bodies to decide by the end of the year on concrete rules and implementation systems for the opening up of their fiber-optic cables to use by others, and it requested that the fees for use be set at or below international levels.

In addition, the Special Committee directed the Ministry of Public Management, Home Affairs, Posts and Telecommunications and the Cabinet Secretariat's IT Policy Office to draw up a set of concrete rules to promote the opening up of underutilized fiber-optic cables ("dark fiber") owned by private sector corporations for use by other enterprises. It is expected that this will produce a major drop in the price of using the backbone network (core fiber-optic cables), which is currently estimated to be four times more expensive in Japan than in the United States or Europe.

Installation of Fiber-Optic Cables in Condominiums

South Korea achieved the rapid spread of high-speed broadband connections because asymmetric digital subscriber line (ADSL) connections were installed in condominiums in a single sweep. But in Japan's case, the law concerning condominium ownership has been interpreted as requiring the agreement of three-quarters of the owners in order for fiber-optic cables to be installed. The Special Committee thus requested the Ministry of Justice, the Ministry of Land, Infrastructure and Transport, and the Ministry of Public Management, Home Affairs, Posts and Telecommunications to clarify the conditions for cable installation so as to make it possible for residential units to be connected in a way that did not substantially affect the condition or utility of the common-use spaces, in keeping with the provisions of the condominium ownership law. This paved the way for installing fiber-optic cables in existing condominiums with the agreement of half of the owners by having the Ministry of Land, Infrastructure and Transport and the Ministry of Public Management, Home Affairs, Posts and Telecommunications produce information on the state of IT-related installation work, offering concrete cases, and by having the Ministry of Justice clarify the interpretation of the conditions for installation. On this basis the IT Strategic Headquarters on September 14, 2001, decided that the procedures for installation of such cables in condominiums would be made clear by the end of that year.

Regulatory Reform and a New Competition Policy System

The Special Committee has also been working toward the construction of a new set of competition policies aimed at achieving further progress in the IT revolution and fully drawing out the latent energy of the private sector. The committee has directed the relevant ministries and agencies to clarify their stance on regulation by approaching the business world for requests and opinions concerning regulations and conducting an overall review of the regulatory system from the perspective of businesses and other users rather than from that of the regulators, the aim being to eliminate unnecessary regulations and sharply reduce the scope of licensing and approval requirements. Through this exercise, the committee hopes to achieve a shift to a new competition policy setup befitting the Internet age and to strengthen the regulatory functions for the promotion of fair competition, thereby allowing the IT revolution to contribute to the reform of the industrial structure and the recovery of Japan's international competitiveness.

On August 30, 2001, Policy Research Council Chairman Asō proposed a concrete set of measures to Takenaka Heizō, the current minister in charge of IT. Through the steps outlined above, the LDP has worked in close cooperation with the prime minister's IT Strategic Headquarters and has guided the government by clarifying specific directions for reform. A new direction for policymaking has thus been achieved in the IT field. We have seen that it is possible to set a path toward reform through political initiative by bringing together legislators familiar with the policies of each of the individual ministries and agencies under the leadership of the LDP's top policymaking officer.

NEW ROLES FOR POLITICIANS

Significance of the System of Senior Vice Ministers

In the process of implementing a new type of policymaking in the IT field, the role of the senior vice ministers as assistants to their ministers was extremely important. The original head of the LDP Special Committee's secretariat is now serving as senior vice minister of economy, trade, and industry in the Koizumi cabinet. Also the senior vice minister of the Cabinet Office and the senior vice minister of public management, home affairs, posts and telecommunications played key roles in maintaining close contact with the LDP Policy Research Council division directors forming the membership of the Special Committee's secretariat; in this way, the Special Committee learned about the policy aims of the government and the specific measures being considered by particular ministries and agencies. On the basis of this information, the Special Committee then drew up its own blueprint for reform, taking into full consideration the need to overcome bureaucratic sectionalism. And by conveying this blueprint to the senior vice ministers, the Special Committee was able to have its proposals accurately reflected within the various ministries and agencies of the government. Politicians took the initiative in setting the major policy directions, transcending the level of the individual bureaucratic organs; this politics-dominated approach made it possible to set an unerring course toward reform and to get policy decisions made speedily.

To a great extent, this success depended on the abilities of the senior vice ministers involved in this process who were familiar with IT policy issues and had experience as LDP division directors and as parliamentary vice ministers. They were also fully aware of the need for coordination to transcend the divisions within the bureaucracy. It was this combination of ability and awareness that made it possible to overcome the tendency of each ministry or agency to fight for its own interests. In short, to achieve a politics-dominated system in the proper sense of the term, it is important that the prime minister and other ministers choose the right people to fill the senior vice ministers' posts.

IT-Driven Changes

The waves of the IT revolution will compel the government to dismantle its existing administrative network and replace it with a new one. This is a demand arising from the emergence of the information market. And those countries that are able to construct a new e-government to enhance their policies and the effectiveness of their implementation will thereby support the competitive impetus of the marketplace.

In the traditional form of public administration in Japan, the bureaucratic division responsible for an industry would build a long-term relationship with that industry, leading to the sharing of detailed information not available to outsiders; the bureaucracy used this as the basis for its policy planning and implementation. Government councils made up of people representing a broader range of interests would check the planning functions of the bureaucracy in advance, and follow-up checking was conducted through internal systems of administrative inspection and auditing, with the legislative branch responsible for the overall checking of the conduct of government through its deliberations on the budget and other proposed legislation. In other words, policy was formed by the bureaucracy within a closed network.

This semimonopolistic system of policymaking was a factor delaying the fundamental reform of systems and policies in the context of the drastically changing market environment of the 1990s. The program of administrative reform has represented an attempt to break away from this arrangement.

The Reagan and Thatcher revolutions in the United States and the United Kingdom and the administrative reform drive of Japan's Nakasone administration, which were all accompanied by deregulation, focused to a large extent on the privatization of state-run enterprises. If we call this the first round of administrative reform, then what has subsequently been happening in each of these countries is a second round, focusing largely on strengthening oversight of the government by the market. This has involved such specific institutional reforms as improving rules on disclosure (freedom of information), introducing a policy evaluation system, no-action letters, and an emphasis on independent commissions. In Japan's 1999 administrative reform, additional internal administrative inspection functions were provided through the strengthening of the cabinet and the implementation of systems of adjusting differences of opinion among ministries and agencies and of disclosure of the activities of government councils.

The second round of administrative reform, by strengthening oversight of the government by the market, has created pressure for institutional reform to allow greater speed and neutrality (i.e., freedom to act without considering particular interests). And now the progress of the IT revolution is generating demand for the next step: going beyond the second round of administrative reform and constructing an e-government. The traditional network, in which information went from individual companies to industry associations and from these associations to the relevant bureaucratic organs, with government councils acting to adjust among conflicting interests, is losing its effectiveness. We are moving to a situation in which it is possible to get much of the information required for policymaking directly from the information market.

Since this information is available to anybody, not just those in the bureaucracy, the age in which the bureaucracy can hold a monopoly on the supply of policy proposals is coming to an end. In other words, the emergence of the digital information market means that there is no longer a need for the bureaucracy to monopolize the process of gathering information, processing it, drafting proposals, adjusting among different interests, and implementing policy. In this context it is becoming possible for think tanks, nonprofit and nongovernmental organizations, and even individual citizens to get involved. What we need to construct now is a new administrative and political network that will take as a given the existence and influence of this information market and that will generate speedy, neutral policy responses to market changes.

In constructing such a network, we need to accelerate the current of administrative decentralization, and at the same time we must not limit the design of e-government at the national and local levels to simply setting up computerized, on-line procedures. Rather, we must build a system of policymaking processes that takes into consideration the emergence of the digital information market.

Politicians must be fully aware of this major coming change in the administrative and political network, and they must assume a central role within the new network, gathering the appropriate information from the open information market, processing it, making proposals, adjusting them, and getting policies approved and implemented.

5

Toward a Fundamental Review of Public Works

Maehara Seiji

During the period of Japan's post–World War II recovery and subsequent era of rapid economic growth, public works such as the building and maintenance of roads and bridges were seen as bringing great benefits to society and boosting the economy. However, once a certain level of infrastructure had been attained, construction of new roads and bridges no longer necessarily contributed to raising industrial productivity and living standards, while the ripple effect on the economy and employment weakened. In recent years, public works have come to be viewed more in terms of the burden they place upon the public purse and on the environment. Voices calling for change can now be heard nationwide.

So intimately connected with the politics, economics, and the social fiber of Japan are public works that their thorough reform would change the very fabric of society. Nevertheless, since only ruin could result were such a step not taken, it was the mission of the Democratic Party of Japan's Committee to Restore Public Works to the People to secure the necessary reforms.

PROBLEMS WITH PUBLIC WORKS PROJECTS

Wasteful Projects

From summer to winter 2000, the three parties (Liberal Democratic Party, New Kōmeitō, and New Conservative Party) of the governing coalition carried out a review of public works projects and cancelled over 200 they deemed wasteful—while leaving extant a wide range of wasteful projects including dams, land reclamation schemes, and airports. Among the projects not singled out for review are some, planned several decades ago, that are still in progress despite having lost all relevance. There are also many projects based on inflated estimates of future demand, assessed according to assumptions valid only in the rapid-growth era, and yet others the purpose of which remains obscure to this day.

Excessive Burden on Public Finance

The combined value of spending on public works by national and local government and special corporations came to more than ¥34 trillion in fiscal year 2000 (ended March 31, 2001). Initial forecasts were in the range of ¥39 trillion but, given the recession and fiscal difficulties of local governments in particular, the final outlay fell well below forecasts. Even so, public works investment amounted to some 6 percent of gross domestic product, a high level compared with that of the industrialized countries of North America and Europe, in which the corresponding figure is generally around 2 percent. Considering that Japan spends roughly half as much as those countries on education and social security, by comparison it remains a "construction state."

Public works projects cost a colossal amount of money. In Japan, there are many cases in which costs are deliberately underestimated at the initial planning stage to make it easier to win authorization for a project, and costs will regularly balloon to several times the original estimate as projects are executed. To support such excessive and inefficient investments, construction bonds have been issued and purpose-specific taxes have been levied for such works as highway construction. The net result of this state-sanctioned benevolence has been to pile up debts that now account for a large chunk of Japan's overall public debt of ¥666 trillion (fiscal year 2001 forecast). With bond repayments now accounting for over 20 percent of the national budget each year, a swift and substantial reduction in public works spending is imperative, not only to protect all members of society, but also to defend their livelihoods.

Environmental Problems

The more than 2,000 dams currently holding back rivers in Japan are destroying the natural environment. Dams obstruct the flow of silt to the sea, thereby exacerbating coastal erosion by waves. To stave off the damage, the coastline is clasped by tetrapods and concrete embankments, to the point where Japan's islands are almost surrounded by concrete. Further, stagnation of the water locked in the dams on rivers and estuaries undercuts water quality, damaging marine resources and ecosystems and resulting in the presence in drinking water of endocrine disrupters, or "environmental hormones." With public works projects inflicting harm on both people and the environment, the well-being and even survival of life forms in these areas may be put at risk should environment-hostile projects be allowed to continue.

Government-Industry Collusion

One of the most damaging aspects of public works projects has been the pivotal role they have played in fostering an "iron triangle" of complicity among politicians, bureaucrats, and businessmen. The resultant steady increase in public works spending, the system of state subsidies, and the practice of designating bidders for public works tenders have made the construction industry the strongest supporter of the governing party which, in turn, has made repeated policy decisions in favor of the industry. The increased spending on public works in the name of economic revitalization since the bursting of the economic bubble is a typical instance. With vested interests seemingly leading politics by the nose, there has developed a widening sense of political alienation among the populace. Powerless against the iron triangle of collusion, citizens have increasingly lost faith and interest in politics, allowing the vested interests to further increase their sway in a vicious spiral that, if unchecked, stands to erode the spirit of democracy, leaving but an empty shell.

Dependence of Local Economies

Japan has been in a serious recession since the economic bubble burst. The consistent response of successive administrations has been to increase public works spending. The situation has become particularly precarious since the failure of the fiscal reform program introduced by the cabinet of Prime Minister Hashimoto Ryūtarō, which was followed by cabinets—of Obuchi Keizō and Mori Yoshirō—that pursued programs of scattershot public spending.

As a result, dependence on excessive public spending has been cultivated nationwide, the only exceptions being a few major cities. At present, even a small measure of fiscal austerity could easily destroy local economies and, were this to happen simultaneously in a number of local areas, the economy and public finances of the entire country could be bankrupted.

With public works spending long having been used to treat economic sluggishness, a large segment of the population has become seriously dependent on such outlays. But if this dependence does not soon cease, local industries will not develop and Japan will be in tatters.

THE INTERMINABLE SYSTEM OF PUBLIC WORKS

How is Japan to kick the public works habit and regain fiscal health? These days even the government and ruling parties concede that wasteful public works spending cannot be allowed to proceed unchecked. To date, reforms have failed to address the cause of the problem, namely, the system that gives rise to wasteful public works projects. Considering, too, that there are said to be over 50,000 projects authorized by the now defunct Ministry of Construction alone, any policy that merely tries to pick off a few of the worst projects can only have a very limited impact. It follows that reforms must be undertaken that will change the system itself.

Public works projects are based on a plan that, after a budget has been drawn up, is implemented as prescribed by law. It would, thus, make sense to change the planning, budgeting, and lawmaking processes that constitute the system's framework, rather than merely cancel a few specific projects.

Public works projects are conceived in accordance with the Comprehensive National Development Plan, which constitutes a blueprint for the entire country, and long-term plans, which lay down specifics for the implementation of projects in each sector.

The Comprehensive National Development Plan

The most fundamental level of public works formulation, this plan is drawn up in accordance with the Comprehensive National Land Development Act. The present Fifth Comprehensive National Development Plan (CNDP), covering the period from 2002 to 2015, is being promoted by the catch phrase, "Promotion of Regional Independence and Creation of Beautiful National Land," which is supposed to signal a change of course away from the traditional land policy focused on development. However, under the influence of the iron triangle, it has been stuffed with a host of even more grandiose construction projects than were previous plans. These include the relocation of capital-city functions, 14,000 kilometers of high-specification trunk roads, two more bridges to link the island of Shikoku to the islands of Honshu and Kyushu (in addition to three existing bridges spanning the Inland Sea), and further development of the experimental super high-speed train known as the maglev (superconducting magnetically levitated vehicle). The costs entailed will far exceed the ¥1,000 trillion figure for the Fourth National Plan. Indeed, it is said that the reason no cost estimates have been published for the current plan is that the outlays are so vast as to be literally incalculable. As long as the iron triangle continues to influence these national plans, the mismatch between theoretical and actual need will continue. Even within government circles there is an awareness of this truth, and a growing number of voices are calling for this plan to be the last.

Within the framework of the National Plan, 16 long-term plans specify public works projects by sector, including roads, flood control, urban parks, sewerage, housing, ports, land improvement, afforestation, airport maintenance, and waste disposal facilities. Here, too, some serious problems exist. Most of these plans were originally launched in the desperate days after World War II, under the Temporary Measures Laws, when Japan was struggling with material and financial shortages but urgently needed to construct roads and other basic infrastructure. But, as the Twelfth Roads Plan is currently being implemented under the very same "emergency measures," on paper at least Japan is in a permanent state of emergency. One might here mention the spectacular growth in spending on flood control and sewerage, the budgets of which have grown at rates 30 percent to 40 percent higher than those of all public works plans combined. Such anomalies, coupled with the colossal scale of the budgets—¥78 trillion for roads, ¥24 trillion for flood control—testify to the fact that plans which cannot possibly be afforded under Japan's current economic and fiscal circumstances have not only been agreed to, but are being implemented.

These plans are drawn up and decided upon by various ministries and bureaus. For instance, road planning is conducted by the Road Bureau of the Ministry of Land, Infrastructure and Transport (MLIT), while flood prevention is handled by the MLIT's River Bureau. With decision making apportioned among ministries, bureaus, and sometimes even among different departments and sections of the same bureau, the vertical division of public works has become structurally embedded in the bureaucratic system, and each segment has developed its own vested interests. This vertically segmented configuration is the reason for which the structure of each plan has scarcely been altered over the decades despite the changing needs of the people. But the biggest problem is the ingrained bureaucratic mentality, which sees it as imperative that budgetary allocations be used up. Thus, as is often said of public works projects, "once they've started, they never stop."

Plans for public works projects often have massive implications for the rights and duties of the general public, as when whole villages are submerged in the course of dam construction, or when people are evicted from their homes to make way for new roads. The projects also place an immense tax burden on the people. While it would follow that in a state which espouses the principle of the rule of law, decisions regarding the plans that are to be implemented should be made by the representatives of the people, in local assemblies or the Diet as appropriate, and that there should be laws to specify how such plans should be implemented, these plans are settled by "cabinet decision" with but a few exceptions. In the case of some categories, including airport maintenance, there is not even a law on the statute books establishing the legitimacy of the enterprise, which fact is one of the major reasons that bureaucrats are in control of public works.

Issues Relating to Individual Laws

Public works projects cannot be implemented just by drawing up a plan. Actual projects are based on individual laws, such as the Road Law or the River Law, which are also seriously flawed.

Complicated Laws Squander Taxpayers' Money

The Road Law carries with it some 30 associated laws, which take effect in combination with various government ordinances, implementation regulations, and official notices that together fill hundreds of pages. Add in all the paperwork involved with the subsidies financing the projects, and virtually no one other than a handful of bureaucrats can grasp the overall picture of what is actually going on. As ever greater areas of legislation have been left to the discretion of bureaucrats, they have increasingly come to dominate the body public. An obscurantist legal framework has turned the world of public works into a black box, while bureaucrats have been permitted to freely decide which projects to implement, teaming up with politicians in the exercise of these far-reaching discretionary powers to create an opaque decision-making apparatus.

Cancellation and Dissent Proscribed

The power of the national government over public works is so overwhelming that there have been calls for devolution of powers, while the monopolization of enterprises that in many cases could be handled by the private sector has led some to call for the application of private finance initiatives that pay due attention to market realities. To date, however, calls for such deregulation have done little to set reform in motion.

The old system of highly centralized authority and total bureaucratic control has been preserved virtually unchanged. The Public Works Law thus still does not involve local assemblies, and there is almost no provision for members of such bodies to publicly express formal opposition or take legal action against projects. Public works have always been determined by laws that include no provision for cancellation.

Not only does the law need simplifying, but devolution and deregulation must be pursued and new legislation created to permit wider participation in projects and the expression of opposition to them.

Essential Fiscal Reforms

Public works projects are broadly of three types, namely, those implemented by the national government directly, by local authorities with the aid of national government subsidies, and by local authorities independently of the national government. The source of funding is taxes (general account, special accounts, etc.) and borrowing (construction bonds, local authority bonds, and funds borrowed from the post office savings and national pension funds under the Fiscal Investment and Loan Program). It is no easy matter to say which project should be carried out using what kind of financing, but at the very least reform is necessary in two main areas.

— Public works: Pork-barrel spending carried out in the name of economic revitalization has only exacerbated the problem. Restoring public finances will require a quantitative spending reduction plan. One possible option would be for central and local government to set a ceiling on their borrowing.

— The system of subsidies: Hitherto, subsidies have caused the management of projects to be split among the administrative strata, with straitjacket standards applied uniformly nationwide, causing unhealthy rivalry among local authorities petitioning the central bureaucracy in Kasumigaseki for subsidies. Local government has been held hostage by this bureaucracy, which uses petitions to strengthen its power.

Recently the system has become further perverted, as the national government has effectively helped pay off local-authority portions of the costs of joint central/local projects by increasing tax grants ex post facto. This has allowed local authorities to enjoy the benefits of projects while shouldering relatively little of the costs entailed, blurring the conceptual link between cost and benefit, and so encouraging local authorities to petition for any project they believe they stand a chance of getting.

EMERGENCY MEASURES TO RESOLVE THE PRESENT CRISIS

Reform of public works is an issue that transcends party politics and concerns the entire citizenry. However, before the system can be reformed and to avert confusion, policies must be established to deal with the projects already under way. This could be done in two stages.

Stage 1: A Complete Review of Ongoing Projects

In the case of dam construction, for example, work should be suspended on projects currently under construction and those planned for the future. Dam building has three major objectives: flood prevention, the supply of irrigation water, and electricity generation. Even the Deliberative Council on Rivers, a government advisory body, has stated that the emphasis in flood prevention has shifted toward mountain preservation and a general emphasis on the environment. As for irrigation and other uses of water, projections for future demand are constantly being revised downward in response to the slowdown in economic growth and population expansion. Meanwhile, liberalization of the electric power industry has exposed the relatively high cost of hydroelectric power. It is hardly surprising that all the major objectives of dam construction now stand in urgent need of review, given that many of the projects under way are based on demand projections 20 to 30 years out of date.

In the areas of expressway and airport construction, it has also been customary to ram through projects based on projections that underestimate construction costs and overestimate demand. Tokyo Bay Aqua Line is a case in point. The initial cost estimate for this ambitious road project was ¥900 billion, but the actual cost weighed in at ¥1.44 trillion, representing a 50 percent cost overrun. The demand projection has proved even more wildly inaccurate, with actual use running below one third of the projected level. More outrageous still, the redemption plan for paying off the loans for the project assumes a continuing increase in traffic, despite the fact that the population of Japan is set to peak in 2007 and then move into decline. The way things are going, it is all too evident that the Japan Highway Public Corporation (JHPC) is well on its way down the same disastrous path traveled by Japan National Railways (JNR), the publicly owned railway company that was privatized in 1987, leaving behind huge debts that are still far from being paid off. The JHPC, together with its sister corporations—the Honshu-Shikoku Bridge Authority, the Metropolitan Expressway Public Corporation, and the Hanshin Expressway Public Corporation—should immediately cease all new construction, be promptly privatized, and make a serious effort to reduce the mountainous debts they have accumulated.

Stage 2: Dealing with the Impact of Project Cancellation

To halt projects now at the planning stage, under construction, or already operative would have a major impact on the areas surrounding the project sites, to the extent that many projects could not realistically be stopped even were it theoretically deemed desirable to do so. There is, thus, the need to establish an environment that would make it possible to halt projects with as little trouble as possible.

Projects under construction generally leave in their wake three main problems when terminated, namely, the questions of what should be done regarding the project funding already spent and facilities already completed; how contractors should be compensated; and how to compensate citizens who have planned their lives on the assumption that projects will go ahead.

Spent Project Funding and Completed Facilities

Inevitably, where implementation costs have already been incurred, the contracting body will have to bear the burden. In most public works projects, costs have already been met through borrowing, and the body in charge of the project is responsible for repaying the debts incurred irrespective of whether the project has been completed. A problem arises, however, when grants from the national government to local governments are involved. According to the Law Relating to Appropriate Execution of Budgets Involving Subsidies Etc., the head of each ministry and agency can revoke the decision (to award a grant) if the body in charge of the enterprise contravenes the contents or conditions of the grant. In such a case, the body in charge of the enterprise must repay the subsidy to the national government with the addition of 10.95 percent per annum. This obligation to repay grants on unfinished projects is one reason that local authorities often feel obliged to carry on with projects that they know to be wasteful. The relevant legislation should be reformed so that the obligation to repay grants does not arise where there is good reason for halting the project.

In much the same way, a flexible approach should be taken regarding facilities already completed, allowing the creative ingenuity of local residents to ensure they are put to optimum use. Where the use of a facility is limited by the terms of the grants awarded, those limitations should be waived, while legal reform is necessary to enable such facilities to be put to alternative uses.

Compensation of Contractors

In terms of compensation to contractors for cancelled projects, the contracting body is currently likely to be found in breach of contract and, therefore, liable for compensation payments. It should, however, be possible to find ways of lightening the load by, for instance, freezing the review period or granting contractors preferential treatment in connection with other project tenders in lieu of compensation payments. Where such arrangements will not suffice to cover the losses sustained by contractors, the outstanding loss will have to be made good by the contracting body, be that the national or a local government, or a partnership thereof.

Compensation of Citizens

The question of compensating citizens is extremely complex and varies in each case. Accepted theory and precedent put severe limits on compensation to citizens. Thus, a decision to construct a dam is not deemed to adversely affect residents, who are not able to claim compensation even when the decision to build a dam has led to the imposition of such building restrictions in the area as a ban on the building of edifices of three or more stories.

However, decades of dam construction have resulted in a great variety of situations, including those involving both individuals who have received compensation and moved to new homes, and those who remain in the area earmarked for flooding. People whose lives have been disrupted by dams have been forced to endure appalling hardship and canceling a dam project would throw up a host of difficult questions. For example, would those who had already received compensation have to repay it? Would those who had not received compensation still be in a position to claim it? And, where projects were suddenly cancelled, there would be even more difficulties regarding how to meet the concerns of those communities the members of which had planned their personal and civic lives on the assumption that some major project would be undertaken nearby.

This is one area which would require legislation that is new and, not bound by existing conventional wisdom, would look at waiving repayment obligations for those who had already received compensation, as well as finding some way of supporting those who had not yet been compensated by, for example, consolation or social support payments.

FUNDAMENTAL REFORM OF THE SYSTEM

Abolition of the Planning System and Creation of a New Legal Framework

The basic planning framework for public works projects is chaotic. There is the CNDP, the National Land Use Plan (NLUP)—based on principles contradictory to those of the CNDP—as well as laws related to the NLUP, namely, the Three Major Urban Areas Development Law, the Law Relating to Local Development and Revitalization, and the Law Relating to Development of Special Regions. While these are the main branches of the planning framework, still more legislation is piled on top, including the Private Participation Promotion Law and the Resort Law. If left untouched, these legal provisions would allow the public works phenomenon to continue forever, so a new legal framework must be established on the basis of decentralization. All 16 of the long-term plans for public works should also be abolished in favor of a system that can flexibly focus public works on the most important areas.

Planning a System to Replace Abolished Public Works Plans

Decentralization of Financial Resources, National Projects

Wasteful public works projects have emerged from a system in which Kasumigaseki bureaucrats have taken charge of project planning and financing, depriving local officials in the affected regions of any awareness of the fiscal burden entailed, while tending toward a uniform national policy that ignores the environment and local culture and history. Were decision-making authority and fiscal responsibility devolved to the regions, the following merits would accrue.

- The views of local residents would be reflected in the selection of projects.
- The vertical segmentation imposed by the Kasumigaseki ministries would end, the expenditure involved in pursuing projects in isolation would be avoided, and synergies could be sought by carrying out mutually complementary projects.
- Local residents could scrutinize the process of bidding for contracts and project implementation.
- Transparency would grow and the involvement of politicians seeking pork-barrel perks decrease.
- Cost reductions would result from the involvement of local residents.

Devolution of public works should start with the reform of the subsidy system. As well as extending vertically segmented administration from the central bureaucracy across the country, the system also leads to massive administrative costs in connection with the labyrinthine application process, and imposes uniform standards nationwide, leading to higher project costs.

To eliminate these evils, a uniform grant system should be established based on integrated subsidies and simple distribution standards. At the same time, a clear distinction should be made between national and local authority projects, to alter the division of roles between central and local government that enables the national government to exercise control even over projects that are supposedly run independently by local authorities.

A clear distinction should be made between public works projects that ought to come under national, and those that should be under local, government jurisdiction. State projects should be strictly limited to those beyond the means of local authorities or that must be handled by the national government because they entail relations with other countries—such as international hub airports, commercial ports, and major trunk roads. Local authorities should carry out all other projects autonomously.

Quantitative Restrictions and Financial Resource Reform

As stated earlier, Japan's spending on public works is excessive, 6 percent to 7 percent of GDP being spent on public works, compared with the roughly 2 percent to 3 percent of GDP in developed Western countries. With Japan's fiscal condition already extremely serious compared with that of those countries, Tokyo must find a way to curb spending.

One way that would work rapidly would be to stipulate a spending reduction target, such as a 30 percent cut over five years. Also, the unlimited issuing of bonds to finance public works should be reduced, and serious consideration given to abolishing construction bonds. Further, the system of earmarking particular revenue sources (such as gasoline tax and vehicle licensing fees) for specific purposes (such as road and airport construction) should be abolished, as it obstructs change in a few budgets at a time when the overall trend is for lower outlays. These revenues could thus be used for whatever purposes a local government deemed necessary.

Getting Elected Assemblies Involved

Although public works projects soak up huge quantities of the taxpayers' money, the law has no provision for significant involvement in these projects by the National Diet or local assemblies. One hears various arguments in favor of the status quo: Project management is better conducted by the executive rather than the legislature; involvement of elected assemblies would open the way to political exploitation of projects, distorting the principle of fairness; and not only is there nothing to stop assemblies from contributing to the planning process, but they already do, being involved in budget hearings. However, political involvement in public works is far more pernicious when conducted in secret than when it is open to scrutiny in a debating chamber. Those who point to budget hearings as a form of democratic involvement are merely engaged in sophistry: The hearings could never take a serious look at the budget for every single dam and road being planned.

Hence none of the arguments against assembly involvement are at all convincing. The absence of elected assemblies from the process of deciding and implementing public works is the biggest impediment to realizing citizen's power of choice over their own affairs. The principle that only the elected representatives of the people should decide how tax revenues are used is fundamental to the modern democratic state, so reform is urgently needed.

Establishing a System of Continuous Review

Some public works projects take decades from launch to completion and, without a system of periodic review, most waste taxpayers' money. A system should be set up that constantly reviews projects to reflect changing socioeconomic conditions. Nor should the review process end with the completion of the project. Another system should be introduced to evaluate the effectiveness and influence of each project on people's lives, so that subsequent projects can be improved with the aid of hindsight.

A law is required—a Basic Law on Public Works—that would transfer funding and decision making to local areas, limiting the scope of directly managed national projects; replace the 16 long-term plans with a single plan; stipulate quantitative reduction targets; require assembly approval of projects; provide for citizen participation; demand project assessment at regular intervals; and call for post-project environmental evaluation and the analysis of cost effectiveness. The result would be a slimming down of the Ministry of Land, Infrastructure and Transport, and a reduction in its authority.

With construction having become the mainstay industry nationwide, most citizens and local authorities have become inured to dependence on the national government and public works. Breaking free of this mindset would require support from the national government and local governments. Giant projects must give way to small-scale ones meeting local requirements, while local communities must develop sustainable industries by setting up community businesses, firming up welfare provisions, and fostering town-village interchanges. Only by developing new industries and employment opportunities can personnel gradually be transferred from the construction industry. This shift in employment patterns will entail the promotion of decentralization and decoupling of income assistance from production promotion policy in primary industries, resulting in the recovery and strengthening of local industry, the development of systems in which volunteers and the elderly can participate, as well as support for both small industries and those that promote environmental recovery. These and other measures will need to be incorporated in another new piece of legislation: a Local Autonomy Support Law.

6

New Policy Challenges in Education

Hase Hiroshi

Prime Minister Koizumi Jun'ichirō, who sees fiscal reform as his greatest political challenge, made famous the story of the Nagaoka fief and the 100 sacks of rice when he mentioned it in his first policy speech to the National Diet in May 2001. At the beginning of the Meiji era (1868–1912), the Nagaoka region was severely impoverished, prompting the lord of a neighboring province to send 100 sacks of rice as assistance. Rather than distribute the rice to the populace, however, the leader of Nagaoka sold it and used the proceeds to build a school to educate his people so that they could generate greater wealth in the future. Koizumi related this tale to make the point that Japan needs to address important long-term tasks that must not be deferred for the sake of short-term gain. The story, however, also illustrates the importance of the nation's investment in education. For many years now, we have been hearing complaints that the Japanese education system has fallen into disrepair, and unless we can clarify appropriate methods and areas for investing in education, those criticisms will continue. In short, we must change the fundamental design of the educational system.

I believe that there are two reasons why this kind of change is needed. First, the educational system has been steadily deteriorating. We have witnessed a simultaneous worsening of school violence, the bullying of fellow students, suicides that result from bullying, children refusing to attend school, disruptive behavior in the classroom, and the increasingly vicious nature of juvenile crime. To these problems we can add the growing lack of a sense of morality and public spirit among young people in Japan and the growing number of children who lack resiliency and quickly "snap." To use Ministry of Education, Culture, Sports, Science and

Technology jargon, the lack of a "zest for living" among Japan's youth is an increasingly grave problem.

The second reason has to do with the development of human resources, on which the nation's very fate hangs. Having completed its process of "catching up" with the West, Japan must focus on scientific and technological creativity if it is to maintain its economic strength and international position. This calls for highly creative human resources—an area in which Japan lags behind other developed countries.

The theme of this chapter, new policy challenges in the field of education, has to do with precisely the need for this sort of radical change. I will begin by exploring the problems and the policy challenges we face, tracing their causes through an analysis of the present state of affairs. One conceivable cause is the country's policies themselves, and I will discuss the kind of policy system that should be developed. Another cause involves the policymaking process, and I will address this mainly in the context of the role of politicians.

EVALUATING EDUCATIONAL POLICY TO DATE

Problems in School Education

Discussions of educational problems generally focus on problems having to do with the method and structure of the education being offered in schools. These include the overemphasis on the acquisition of knowledge and rote learning, which has led to a lack of emphasis on the development of creativity and humanity, and the Education Ministry's top-down administration of school management, which has given rise to a highly administrative, standardized education. The present structure can only be regarded as stifling of individuality and maladapted to present-day educational needs.

If, however, we consider things in the historical context from Meiji times onward, it is clear that this school education policy was not always misguided. When Japan began modernizing, it lagged behind the West in every way—politically, culturally, economically, and scientifically—and to catch up with Western developed countries, it needed to eradicate illiteracy and develop a workforce equipped with a stable base of technical and practical skills by means of education skewed toward (or, as believed at the time, "valuing") knowledge. And to ensure such a workforce on a national level, there was no alternative to standardized education. This was also in keeping with the ideal of equal education for all. We can see the overemphasis on standardized scores that is often criticized today as a byproduct of that past overemphasis on knowledge-based education.

This type of state-led, centrally controlled education was suited to an educational system aimed at realizing the national policy of modernization. After World War II, as well, Japan maintained an educational system responsive to the economic demands of the time. As a result, the country was lauded both at home and abroad for having succeeded in catching up with the West. The problem, however, is that the educational policy and educational system that were appropriate in the past can no longer meet the needs of the present. In short, they have outlived their usefulness.

Problems of Teachers, Parents (Family), and Community

Today's educational problems are not limited to school education. Problems in this area alone cannot adequately explain why an educational policy and system consistently maintained since the 1950s began to manifest a cluster of problems all at once and in such an explosive manner in the 1980s. It is reasonable to conclude that the compounding of various factors, particularly those related to the major social changes that began to take place in the 1980s, brought about this critical situation. As one significant contributing factor, I would note the decline of the educational power of the "educators"—including teachers, parents (family), and community—since the 1980s. I believe that this decline in educators inevitably made learning less fun and brought about a weakening of the rules (an increasingly laissez-faire policy, letting children have their way), thus helping to cause this critical decline in the educational system.

Why did this decline in educators occur? People tend to cite standardized education skewed toward the acquisition of knowledge, but I think that argument misses the mark. Instead, I believe there are a number of interrelated reasons. One, which I will examine in detail in my discussion of the policymaking process, is the effect of the ideological conflict between the Education Ministry and the Nihon Kyōshokuin Kumiai (Nikkyōso, or Japan Teachers' Union). Another is the intelligentsia's misguided importation of liberal democracy, and particularly their emphasis on a laissez-faire approach not based on discipline, and on human rights without regard for coexistence. They repudiated the education—mainly moral education—carried out by parents, family, and the community as being unwarranted interference that was incompatible with respect for the individual. In this context, the decline in educators was exacerbated by parents' lack of interest in the character formation of their children and the consequent culture of extreme dependence on schools.

EVALUATING POLICYMAKING IN THE FIELD OF EDUCATION

The policymaking process with regard to education and the actors involved in it has changed over time. We must therefore evaluate this process in the context of the respective periods in question.

Conflict between the Education Ministry and Nikkyōso

For some time after Japan was relieved of the Occupation government following World War II, the Education Ministry's top-down administrative system shaped educational policy. Prefectural and municipal boards of education were not allowed independent status, and Nikkyōso was the only opposition force. Confrontation with the ministry was especially fierce in regard to issues of school administration and the teaching staff system, such as teacher performance assessment and the senior teacher system, with Nikkyōso seeking to represent teachers as laborers. However, it never managed to be anything more than an outside pressure group that tried to exert influence on the policymaking process.

Meanwhile, the ruling Liberal Democratic Party's (LDP's) "law-and-order clique" in the Diet was the main player in policy formation, doing its utmost to come up with measures to counter Nikkyōso. Its role was limited, however, and the Education Ministry generally played the decisive policy role on all other issues. This unproductive ideological conflict within the supply side of education—i.e., between the ministry and Nikkyōso—was never supported by the public, and the mutual mistrust between these two sides left them functionally unable to cope with any real educational issues. In later years, Nikkyōso, facing a shrinking membership and beset by internal divisions, lost its erstwhile power as it sought reconciliation with the ministry.

The Emergence of the "Education Clique"

The turmoil on university campuses in the 1970s saw the emergence of an LDP "education clique" of legislators interested in education. By and large, clashes between the education clique and the Education Ministry were limited to peripheral issues; generally, the two cooperated to gain budget allocations in a time of fiscal austerity. The education clique's main role was to oppose Diet cliques linked with other government agencies. This phenomenon was not limited to educational relations but extended to all government agencies. What we should note here is that analysis of LDP-bureaucracy leadership struggles in the policymaking process in different policy areas is meaningless. The fact is that the key struggles were between "partial governments" comprised of the respective government agencies and the related LDP cliques dealing with each specific policy issue. What is more, the Diet cliques were more interested in gaining budget funds after policy decisions had been made than they were in being part of the policymaking process. In regard to education, for example, the education clique was most keen to win budget funds for private schools from kindergarten through university. Like other government agencies, the Education Ministry strengthened its culture of upholding vested interests and, partly because of its conflict with Nikkyōso, was too timid to take the initiative in reform.

Policy Formation

Since 1952, the Central Council for Education under the Education Ministry has been active in policy formation. A new kind of policymaking process began in 1984, however, during the administration of Nakasone Yasuhiro, with the passage of legislation establishing a National Council on Educational Reform with a three-year mandate. This marked the start of educational reform led by the cabinet and the new council. The policymaking method adopted was for the council to distance itself from both the Education Ministry and the LDP education clique, exclude education scholars as far as possible, and rely mainly on industry representatives for advice. What we should note here is the attempt to shift the initiative from the supply side—the Education Ministry, Nikkyōso, and other education service providers—to the consumer side—industry and the general public, including parents. The consumer side stepped up to address reform because it felt that reform could no longer be left to the supply side. Behind this move was discontent over the fact that educational decline had already begun to spread and that educational circles were not responding to the human-resource development needs of industry or of the nation as a whole. Therefore, this revolutionary change sought to do more than simply tinker with the power structure; it aimed at a major policy shift from a controlling, standardized education to a liberalized education.

The Council's Influence on Policy

The policy and power-structure shifts that the National Council on Educational Reform hoped to put in place were thwarted, but its work had a dramatic effect on subsequent educational policy and the policymaking process. In terms of policy, although a shift to liberalization through the introduction of the principle of market competition that the council had wished was not realized, diversification of education also received a strong push, as seen in the introduction of the five-day school week, unified secondary schools combining middle and high school, measures enabling gifted students to skip a year, the establishment of elective courses (where students can choose from a wide range of subjects they would like to study, including either general subjects or specialized subjects) at the high school level, diversification of university entrance examinations, and the introduction of interdisciplinary-study periods (where students develop learning and life skills through classroom lessons focusing on an interdisciplinary approach to subjects). In regard to the policymaking process, through the Central Council for Education, the Education Ministry began to actively address educational reform and introduced the principle of competition to employment conditions for university professors. Basically, these reforms were undertaken in response to the four reports issued by the National Council on Educational Reform during its three years of operation.

The LDP education clique also began to take an active part in educational policy, leading the ministry in policy. For example, it was the education clique that proposed such reforms as a revision of the Fundamental Law of Education, the modification of the 6-3-3-4 system, the encouragement of smaller classes, the introduction of measures to ensure the quality of the teaching staff, and the enhancement of moral education. It is especially noteworthy that politicians took the lead in getting volunteer and other community service activities added to the curriculum, prevailing over a reluctant ministry. The cabinet, the Education Ministry, and education-clique politicians have now begun to work together to promote educational reform. Since the decline of Nikkyōso, most opposition parties have also taken a positive approach. The Democratic Party of Japan, the largest opposition party, basically agreed with the introduction of community service activities, an example that can be regarded as typical of that party's cooperative stance.

To be certain, far from all of the reforms proposed by the council were realized, since it was unable to inject the principle of free competition into education as a whole. Nevertheless, the consumer side was provided with more diverse educational options, so that in consumers' eyes, something close to liberalized education was achieved. That achievement deserves high praise. The National Council on Educational Reform advocated a third great educational reform—the first great reform being the Meiji Restoration, and the second following the end of World War II. The work begun by the council has continued up to the present and is truly worthy of being called the third great reform. It also deserves praise as a revolutionary change undertaken not at a time of political revolution or national emergency, but during a period of relative calm.

Approach to Educational Reform Today

Above I have given a fairly positive and optimistic assessment of the National Council on Educational Reform, but in these early years of the 21st century, educational reform is still a work in progress. The framework is now in place, but the true test will be how it is understood and incorporated in the classrooms. I have already noted that the reforms introduced so far owe a great deal to the initiative of the consumer side, the general public. As the representatives of the people, politicians were sensitive to this trend and responded with their own reform proposals. In other words, the series of reforms that began with the council's work had its origin in the dysfunctional state of the supply side, and was then propelled by the subsequent response by the politicians to consumers' demands.

Politicians have begun taking a more active part in policymaking in all areas of Japanese politics in recent years. In the area of education, a new type of politician has become active, different from past members of the education clique. Unlike those politicians who were preoccupied with gaining budget funds for education and amending the tax provisions relating to education, politicians of this new breed boldly discuss and seek to put into practice educational principles and policies on the basis of their own convictions and experience. More than members of other Diet cliques, they openly proclaim their principles and policies and translate these into actual measures. The aforementioned introduction of community service activities affords a good example of this approach. Another example is a change in the conditions for licensing teachers to require practical training in nursing care. To achieve this, concerned politicians formed a parliamentary group and submitted a Diet members' bill despite the Education Ministry's opposition. The Soccer Promotion Lottery (Soccer Lottery) Law, aimed at securing funds for promoting sports activities in local communities, also resulted from a bill submitted by Diet members. The Education Ministry had balked for fear of the harmful effect soccer lotteries might have on young people. Nonetheless, this law was in fact highly attractive to the ministry, which has had little policy funding to use freely, and its passage helped make the education clique still stronger.

We should note here that for members of today's education clique, unlike the Diet cliques associated with, say, construction or agriculture, education is not an issue that is usually tied to votes or fund-raising, except in connection to kindergartens. For this reason, the education clique is shaped by members' individual convictions and interests rather than support groups in their constituencies. Also, many of the clique's key members have served as minister of education and have subsequently remained actively interested in educational affairs. Few members fit the mold of the core members of other Diet cliques: politicians who have headed the relevant division of the LDP's Policy Research Council, served as director and chairman of the relevant Diet committee, and been parliamentary vice minister of the relevant ministry. Thus, the education clique is a loose grouping with no hierarchy or unwritten code, and its members are relatively unlinked by interests. For this reason, it also has fewer members and less cohesive force than other Diet cliques. This is not unrelated to the education clique's comparative weakness when it comes to campaigning. Moreover, from the perspective of the Education Ministry, the field of education is fairly well insulated from politics and there is little policy overlap with other government agencies, so very few issues require liaison with other agencies. As a result, the ministry has seen no need to cultivate its own Diet clique.

In terms of members' backgrounds, the present members tend to come from the Mori and Etō-Kamei factions of the LDP, and many have been involved with education, especially physical education and sports. There are now few second-generation Diet members or former members of the Waseda University oratorical society—two traits that were prominent among the members of the education clique in the 1970s and 1980s.

It strikes me that the type of politician found in the education clique today is well suited to carrying out reform, since reform means breaking down vested interests; politicians with particular interests may have a great store of specialized knowledge, but because of their ties to vested interests they find it difficult to undertake reform. And in fact, the politicians now active in the field of education have begun to put forward a variety of proposals for educational reform. Before turning to the role politicians should play in political reform more broadly, I would like to summarize the direction of educational reform that my colleagues and I have envisaged.

APPROPRIATE EDUCATIONAL POLICIES FOR A NEW AGE

In promoting educational reform, we need to articulate the framework of a policy system in which individual policies can be clearly identified. Unless we do, it will be difficult to carry out prior and ex post facto evaluation of both individual policies and the reform package as a whole. Here, I will discuss the policy system in terms of two axes. One is the vertical axis of time, which expresses the changes in an individual's school record with advancing age, from kindergarten through elementary, middle, and high school and on to university and graduate school. This is the school record axis. The other is the horizontal axis of place and space, which expresses an individual's relationships with the educational actors and forums that impact on him or her—family, community, and industry. This can be called the societal axis. In the relationships between the two axes, we see that as individuals age (school record), they deepen their connections first with family, then community, and finally industry; as each set of connections deepens, the earlier ones weaken. This is the relationship between the school record axis and the societal axis.

Educational Reform Proposals—The School Record Axis

The aim of future educational reform is to develop highly creative human resources. This is essential if Japan is to continue developing as a nation based on scientific and technological creativity, the necessary condition for maintaining its economic strength and international position. This means aiming to maximize people's skills and individuality. The goal should not be an educational system designed to mass-produce human resources with uniform skills, as in the catching-up period, but one that seeks to develop human resources equipped with a highly creative "new" scholastic ability, defined by the Education Ministry as the ability to identify and solve problems by oneself. As specific policies to this end, I propose rethinking the present 6-3-3-4 single-track school system and replacing it with a multitrack system. The main points of this proposal are summarized below.

Expansion of the Elective Course and Credit-System High Schools

Multitrack education can be advanced through the expansion of the elective course, which allows students to choose among general and specialized subjects, at the high school level and of credit-system high schools. The elective course in particular can be expected to result in schools that seek to accentuate their own distinctive characteristics. We should expand the number of such schools so that there is at least one in each school district.

Expansion of Unified Secondary Schools

Originally, unified secondary schools—those combining both middle and high school—were designed to eliminate the ill effects of high school entrance examinations, but they led to the emergence of "entrance-exam elite" schools. To strengthen the multitrack system, unified secondary schools should offer diverse special features. Some might be "elite schools" for students intending to go on to university, while others might concentrate on English education, on science education (giving credits for university-level courses, for example), on physical education, on the arts, on "human education" (i.e., paying attention to providing education in keeping with individual students' rate of progress over the six-year period), or on the thorough provision of a basic education.

Rebuilding of Elite Education through Unified Secondary Schools

In connection with the expansion of unified secondary schools, it is necessary to rebuild elite education so that it once again reflects its original aim of developing able human resources that contribute to and are respected by society. Nowadays, the so-called elite are thought of as no more than clever people skilled at getting their own way. We must nurture leaders of society endowed with public spirit if we are to build a society replete with the volunteer spirit, in which good citizens and good neighbors are respected. This is critical to the development of a mature civil society, constituted of citizens who can voluntarily and independently rise to meet the challenges facing them, without relying on the government.

Improvement of Class Management

In addition to improving schools themselves by expanding unified secondary schools and credit-based high schools, measures at the classroom level will encourage multitrack education. Specific steps include encouraging small classes of 20 or so students for major subjects and the promotion of team teaching, as well as allowing gifted students to skip a year and spreading the system of study based on students' actual mastery of subject matter (the latter two being modes of study that emphasize individuality).

Measures to Promote Effective Secondary School Reform

As we implement the above-noted proposals for the promotion of multitrack secondary education emphasizing individuality and skills, there are a number of points that will require attention. First, to overcome the negative aspects of a multitrack education, which is characterized by early decisions regarding students' career paths, students must be allowed to change their career paths partway through. Second, switching from the 6-3-3-4 system to a 5-4-3-4 system represents only another kind of single-track system and is meaningless. Third, freedom to choose among schools is an important component of the multitrack system, but it is necessary to draw the line at the kind of liberalization based on the principle of market competition advocated by the National Council on Educational Reform, which could create conditions in which schools might go broke at any time. Nor can I support a voucher system, since schools would fail unless they attracted a critical mass of students. Still, the competitive principle as generally understood is essential, and further study should be given to such potential measures as allowing the achievements of highly motivated teachers to be reflected in their salaries, creating an appropriate system to allow the removal of problem teachers, enhancing the system of continuing training for highly motivated teachers, adjusting the funding given to schools on the basis of performance, and in this connection, establishing an independent body to evaluate schools' performance.

University Entrance Examination Reform

Reform of university entrance examinations, which at present are skewed toward the regurgitation of knowledge, is essential to the expansion of unified secondary schools. For this reason, we should study such measures as setting up an independent evaluation body to assess which universities are attempting to attract creative human resources through imaginatively designed entrance exams and scaling budget allocations accordingly. And in view of the tendency to rely too heavily on written tests in order to minimize costs and time requirements, we should also consider providing grants for the expansion of "admissions office" entrance exams, which emphasize essays and interviews.

University Reform

In recent years, national universities have attracted increasing criticism for not living up to their original goal of transmitting research findings to society and for failing to turn out enough useful human resources. I cannot discuss national university reform in detail here, but I would like to emphasize the need to remove the internal and external controls on national universities and to restore their vigor by making them independent administrative corporations. The ills associated with overregulation—the inflexibility of the higher-education budget and the difficulty of accessing external sources of research funding, for example—are widely acknowledged. There is an urgent need for measures such as allowing national universities to set their own budget priorities, or shifting the initiative for university administration from the faculty council to an executive council headed by the president.

To facilitate this, we should consider establishing a system of external evaluation and budget prioritization based on such evaluations, as well as the full-scale introduction of fixed-term contracts for faculty. Thought should also be given to devising a system whereby budget funds can be provided in accordance with national policy priorities, as by strategically allocating funds to key institutions in fields of research considered likely to develop on a global scale or to be globally competitive. However, it would be difficult to devise such a system if national universities were fully privatized. For this reason, too, converting national universities into independent administrative corporations is desirable.

University-Industry Collaboration

Strengthening collaboration between universities and business will also lead to university reform. There is an urgent need for more technology licensing organizations to match industry needs with university research findings. We should also reform the university personnel system so as to promote university-industry joint research and enable professors to serve concurrently as company directors. In this connection, universities should be encouraged to develop the ability to launch their own business ventures.

Educational Reform Proposals—The Societal Axis

The aim of educational reform in regard to the societal axis is to improve the educational power of family and community in order to deal with bullying, refusal to attend school, and other aspects of educational decay.

The basic intent of this revival of societal educational power is to enhance children's sense of morality and public spirit, to give them a sense of the significance and joy of learning, and to equip them with a "zest for living" through greater collaboration among family, community, and school.

Revival of the Educational Power of the Family

Such phenomena as the spread of the nuclear family and the increase in two-income families has created a situation in which the disciplining of children, traditionally undertaken chiefly by the family, has become inadequate. Strengthening services that target parents, such as child-rearing courses, counseling, and the establishment of public consultation centers, is important, but the involvement of and follow-up by the community as a whole are also necessary. Welfare officers, who can be described as the community's public volunteers, are doubling as juvenile officers, but we need to put in place dedicated juvenile officers so as to strengthen support for young families and take other measures to keep nuclear families from becoming isolated from the community. We should also consider a system allowing older people and younger married couples to help one another, as through the use of "eco-money," currency used only within a local community. Community relations could be improved if a system existed under which members could help each other. Enhancement of after-school child-care centers is needed, as well; due in part to issues over which government agency has jurisdiction, the current budget allocations are inadequate. Clearly, the Ministry of Health, Labor, and Welfare and the Education Ministry should share jurisdiction and work together to promote better after-school child care. Moreover, in keeping with their own long-term enlightened self-interest, the companies that employ parents should recognize their social responsibility to cooperate. In sum, a revival of the educational power of the family depends on cooperation between the state, businesses, and the community to make things easier for parents.

Revival of the Educational Power of the Community

The key to supporting ailing schools and alleviating today's educational decay is the community at the level of the school district. Society at the local level interacts as a community in various aspects of daily life. In order to sustain that community, the sound development of the children is essential, and it is therefore in the community's own interest to work toward alleviating today's educational decay.

I believe that bringing the community's volunteer activities into the schools by making school-based community service activities compulsory is the most effective way of reviving the community's educational power. At present, simply teaching children about morality and public spirit in the classroom is ineffective. Hands-on welfare activities and other social-service activities make children realize that they are useful and give them a "zest for living." Making schools the nucleus of such activities, however, places too great a burden on them; the community must play the leading role.

There has been some criticism of the idea of making volunteer activities—which by nature are independent, unpaid, and socially oriented—compulsory in schools. I would like it understood that the objectives of community service activities are to nurture the next generation of those who will take part in volunteer activities and thus rectify the national culture of overreliance on government to solve problems, and to cultivate true citizens who think about what they can do for government, rather than what government can do for them, and act accordingly. Underlying this proposal is the idea that a society with vigorous volunteer and nonprofit activities is the ideal for the 21st century. Here again, promoting volunteer activities requires the involvement of the community as a whole, including parents and businesses.

Charter (Community) Schools

School education in which schools and the community offer hands-on social experience together, and thus social-education activities, represents a partial "fusion of school and society." Efforts to bring about this kind of school-society fusion should be further promoted at the elementary and middle-school levels. In some communities, such initiatives are already under way. The schools that most fully incorporate the idea of school-society fusion are the charter schools that originated in the United States, which the National Commission on Educational Reform calls "community schools." The community, business, and ordinary residents together determine the school's educational principles and curriculum and have the school certified on the basis of a charter with the municipality or prefecture. Of course, these schools receive fiscal assistance in the same way as public schools; they are, in effect, publicly established, privately administered schools. What is important is to effectively shift the board of education's authority to make personnel decisions to the school principal, make use of the talents of the community, and ensure that the community monitors school administration. Since the community's educational power is still inadequate, it is too soon to establish such schools nationwide, but we have reached the stage where model schools should be set up as a national policy.

Seen from another perspective, the restructuring of schools using the revival of the community's educational power as a catalyst is actually the decentralization of education. To local educational institutions accustomed to waiting for directions from the central government, decentralization from above would simply lead to chaos; but decentralization can be highly effective if it is grounded in the enhancement of community volunteer activities.

Amendment of the Fundamental Law of Education

The educational reforms discussed so far have to do with enhancing what the Education Ministry calls "education for the heart." This phrase often leads opponents to charge simplistically that educational reform itself represents a reversion to prewar moral education or to parochialism. Because such arguments have a certain plausibility, they block the progress of reform proposals. It is critical that we make it quite clear that there cannot and will not be any regression to the prewar disregard for individual rights and, on this basis, that we gain public understanding of and a national consensus on precisely what is meant by enhancing "education for the heart." Without a national consensus, there is a very real danger that, as back in the days of conflict between the Education Ministry and Nikkyōso, new systems will be watered down at the operational level. This indicates the importance of public oversight at the operational level.

For this reason, I suggest amending the Fundamental Law of Education. The law as it stands says nothing about the importance of the community's role in education. Thus, it places no weight on Japan's traditions and provides no image of Japanese people and society for the 21st century. More importantly, in its overemphasis on freedom, the law fails to indicate the importance of discipline. True freedom can exist only in the context of appropriate discipline. Unless we debate these points properly and build a national consensus, I fear that the "third great educational reform" will be ineffectual. Just as we are debating the amendment of the Constitution of Japan, I propose a debate on the amendment of the Fundamental Law of Education.

POLICYMAKING AND THE ROLE OF POLITICIANS

As the field of education has changed during the postwar period, so too has the role of politicians in education-related policymaking. As I have discussed, we are now facing the need for a monumental shift in educational policy, the "third great educational reform." What role can politicians play? And how can they engage effectively in the policymaking process so as to fulfill that role?

As already noted, since the time of the National Council on Educational Reform, the LDP education clique and the Education Ministry, under cabinet leadership, have worked together to formulate education policy. This, I think, represents the correct basic direction. Under the Obuchi and Mori administrations, the National Commission on Educational Reform was set up in 2000 as a private advisory body to the prime minister. There is one major difference between the National Council on Educational Reform and the more recent National Commission on Educational Reform, however: Whereas the establishment of the council was subject to strong opposition by the education clique, the creation of the commission enjoyed strong education-clique support.

Both the council and the commission were established as cabinet initiatives. Why, then, did the education clique support the commission? One reason was that the prime minister at the time the commission compiled its interim and final reports was Mori Yoshirō, who was the "boss" of the education clique. In short, care was taken to get the education clique on board beforehand. Another reason was that the bulk of the content of the commission's reports echoed ideas already put forward by the education clique. And as a background factor, we cannot overlook the fact that around the time of the council, the Education Ministry's power began to wane. This can be seen as a sign of the council's efficacy. As I have already noted, after the council, the public supported cabinet-led educational reforms, which effectively signified the public's refusal to let the Education Ministry take the lead in the reform process. I think that reflection on the council experience has facilitated the progress of cabinet-led educational reform. Within the context of cabinet-led educational policymaking, politicians should collaborate with the cabinet (not forming issue-based "partial governments" with the respective government agencies) to push forward reform proposals. This type of process should be applied not only to education policymaking, but to other policy areas as well.

In addition, in view of the nature of educational reform, it is desirable that bills be submitted first to the House of Councillors (Upper House) rather than the House of Representatives and be subjected to thorough debate as a long-term national educational plan. The significance of the bicameral legislature has been questioned, but in the case of educational reform, which requires lengthy debate and both careful and bold solutions, I think the Upper House has a major role to play, given that its members have six-year terms and that it aspires to "politics of reason," reflecting the will of the people.

JAPAN'S POLICYMAKING SYSTEM AS A WHOLE

The Ruling Party–Cabinet Relationship

Thus far, I have concentrated on the policymaking process in the field of education and outlined the impressive achievements of the cabinet-led educational reform process. Here, I would like to discuss how Japan's policymaking process as a whole might be shifted to a similar cabinet-led system. The 1990s in Japan have been called the "lost decade," as calls for reform not only in education, but in all fields—the economy, industry, the bureaucratic system, social security, and so on—made little progress. Analysis of the reasons for this lack of progress will be helpful to understanding what sort of changes are required.

One reason reform has not progressed much has to do with the phenomenon of what I have called "partial governments"—specifically, the way in which "partial governments" in each field of government administration craft policy. This was not a problem when Japan was enjoying steady economic growth, but now that growth has stopped, the system has become unworkable. At a time when anticipated future budget outlays have to be closely reviewed and policy priorities set, coordination among government agencies is imperative. Cabinet-led policy coordination is the minimum necessary condition. In view of this, the recent creation of the Cabinet Office and the establishment of the Council on Economic and Fiscal Policy as a result of a series of amendments of laws dealing with government organization are steps in the right direction. Whether they are effective will depend on whether they operate as intended.

Even if cabinet-led policy coordination can be achieved, however, a serious concern still remains, namely, the recent tendency of the LDP, and the ruling coalition as a whole, to excessively involve itself with policy. With the end of the so-called 1955 system, whereby the LDP had maintained a solid majority of seats in the Diet from 1955 through 1993, the central government agencies, including the cabinet, lost the ability to carry out policy coordination across agencies. Probably in reaction to this new environment, the LDP's Policy Research Council began to involve itself with government agencies and took the initiative in policymaking. In the present period of coalition government, some opinion leaders even regard meetings of the ruling parties' top policymakers as having equal weight to the cabinet. In this bipolar situation, the cabinet and the coalition parties frequently clash over basic policy, and coordinating policy with the coalition is often laborious. The biggest problem is that the LDP, which is playing the central role in the policy process, is too closely tied to special interests and the groups representing them and thus cannot solidify opinion within the party. It is eminently clear that the LDP cannot play the main role in carrying reforms forward.

In view of this situation, I strongly advocate amending the Constitution to stipulate direct election of the prime minister. The object of introducing such a system would be to invest the prime minister with national authority. Without such authority, I believe, neither the prime minister nor the cabinet can exercise true leadership and thus cannot overcome the vested interests in the old system, a process which is essential for reforms. First, when a party leader is elected in Japan, the elected candidate's promise is not viewed as a party promise. Second, because Japan has adopted the parliamentary cabinet system, the prime minister is formally chosen by Diet vote. In other words, there is no direct involvement of the public in the election process, and as a result, generations of prime ministers have been dependent on ruling-party (especially LDP) Diet members and faction leaders. Basically, there is no distinction between the prime minister and faction leaders in terms of authority. This means that the prime minister cannot advance his own policies or push through reforms based on his own convictions in the face of opposition forces within his party. Thus, the party's policymaking bodies, which are headed by faction leaders, exercise their power extraterritorially, and the prime minister is forced to engage in policy coordination with them from the start. The reason that the United Kingdom, which like Japan has a parliamentary cabinet system, does not engage in this kind of "bipolar politics"—and the reason that party heavyweights all join the cabinet—is that in U.K. general elections, party leaders are in the forefront, which in effect amounts to direct election of the prime minister. In other words, the party leader's pledges are party pledges, and if that party takes power, they become the prime minister's pledges. In Japan, where there is little sense of the head of the party being the leader of the party and of voting for parties as such, the adoption of a complete single-member-constituency system for general elections would render it impossible to replicate the United Kingdom's de facto direct-election system.

Direct election of the prime minister would mean that a party's very fate rested on the outcome of the election, with prime ministerial candidates' pledges being their parties' pledges. In other words, through direct elections, prime ministerial candidates' pledges would guide and coalesce their parties' pledges. And the introduction of direct elections would probably lead to party heavyweights, policy experts, and leaders of Diet cliques emerging together as candidates for cabinet posts. This would ameliorate the present system of bipolar politics.

Prior Review by the Ruling Party

Direct election of the prime minister, although an improvement, is not sufficient in and of itself to do away completely with the current bipolar structure. It is also necessary to improve the system of prior review of bills and other measures by the ruling party. When cabinet bills are drafted, the ruling party customarily reviews them, but the time allotted is brief and government agencies' input is limited, resulting in a highly unsatisfactory process. Moreover, the Diet committee deliberation that follows LDP review is formalistic because of tight party discipline. Given this situation, it would be more effective if we were to take advantage of the recently devised system of parliamentary secretaries and senior vice ministers by having them serve concurrently as party division directors and deputy directors of the Policy Research Council and be involved in the drafting of cabinet bills from the start. And if party review were conducted simultaneously with the policymaking process in government agencies, I believe this would lead not only to more effective collaboration between politicians and bureaucrats in the policymaking process, but also to the improvement of politicians' policymaking skills, thus killing two birds with one stone.

Most importantly, we should abolish the final decision by the party (in the case of the LDP, the decision by the General Council) in relation to policy, leaving only the cabinet decision. In other words, we should strengthen the party cabinet system, making the cabinet decision the ruling party's highest and final policy decision. The present situation of bipolar policy formulation by the party and the cabinet leads to postponing or watering down needed reforms. This process should be consolidated immediately and, as mentioned above, the focal point should be the cabinet. I should note that this idea means getting rid of the controversial *prior* review by the ruling party (that is, prior to the cabinet decision), while not repudiating ruling party review itself. If we look at the example of Germany, there is vigorous ruling party review, but it is conducted *after*, not before, legislation has been submitted to parliament.

In my view, the LDP Policy Research Council should be retained, with parliamentary secretaries and senior vice ministers serving concurrently as division directors and deputy directors. They would see that division decisions were debated in cabinet and endorsed through cabinet decisions. (At that point, a distinction would be made between matters requiring strong party discipline and those necessitating only loose discipline, for reasons given below.) This, coupled with direct election of the prime minister (direct election serving to promote unification of policy formulation within the cabinet), would permit party heavyweights—including the chairman of the Policy Research Council—and policy experts to join the cabinet en masse. Cabinet ministers would also evolve from being mere spokespeople for government agencies to becoming true ministers of state, exercising comprehensive and strategic leadership of government agencies. This is what the Constitution sees as the primary duty of cabinet members.

The Ruling Party-Diet Relationship

Thus far, I have been discussing the role of politicians in terms of the relationship between the ruling party and the cabinet, but we must also reconsider their role in terms of the relationship between the ruling party and the Diet. There is no doubt that Diet members will be assessed on their performance in getting members' bills passed and amending cabinet bills. In terms of the future role of politicians in policy decisions, however, given Japan's present legislative conditions—inadequate attention to upgrading politicians' policymaking skills or to ensuring adherence to the proposition that new legislation supersedes old, and the need for advance coordination of proposed legislation with related laws—we should change the Diet so that, to begin with, members' amendments to bills submitted by the cabinet, especially those originating with bureaucrats, become commonplace. Working toward increasing the number of bills submitted by members should be the next step. We must not forget that change in the policymaking process is also Diet reform.

In this connection, improving opposition parties' ability to crystallize opinion and formulate policy is highly desirable. To enhance opposition parties' policymaking skills, treasury funds should be made available specifically for opposition parties to gather information, as in the case of the United Kingdom's shadow cabinet system. In addition, a system of government agencies seconding personnel to both ruling- and opposition-party staff should be introduced to provide information and follow up on policy proposals, with especially generous support to opposition parties.

Looking to the future, we may need to designate a way to encourage the practice of Diet members submitting bills. I would like to suggest four points to create the necessary environment. First, Diet members' policy staff should be upgraded. Diet members' policy staffers should be made Diet staff members, and after a certain amount of training, they should be assigned to parties and pooled according to policy area. Seconding of bureaucrats to political parties would also contribute to this. Second, the conditions regarding the number of Diet members required to submit a members' bill should be relaxed. Individual Diet members have the right to legislate, even though the Constitution does not regulate it, so the Diet Law should be amended to allow even one Diet member to submit a bill. (I have already submitted a bill to this effect to the LDP in the House of Councillors.) The danger of self-serving bills can be averted adequately by reviewing bills at the time of submission to determine whether they will be referred to the Diet. Third, in connection with the above points, a regular day should be set for reviewing members' bills to determine whether they will be formally referred to the Diet for deliberation. Giving priority to cabinet bills is natural in a parliamentary cabinet system, but for this very reason, it is essential to set aside one day a week for reviewing members' bills. These three conditions represent the bare minimum required to encourage members' bills. A fourth condition is the abolition of the institutionalized system whereby party factions give their approval to the bills before they are submitted to the Diet. Within this particular system, party discipline is excessive to the point of inhibiting the politicians' legislative rights.

One additional problem in this connection is the timing of the imposition of party discipline by the ruling parties, and particularly the LDP. Traditionally, party discipline is imposed before questioning when a bill is in committee, which means that even if good policy proposals emerge from committee questioning, the bill is seldom amended, so that committee questioning has been more or less reduced to a formality. We should shift to a system of imposing party discipline when a bill is voted on in committee, *after* the questioning process. This is the method followed in Germany, which like Japan has strong party discipline, and we should learn from this example. I believe that if we amend the policy process in this way, questioning by all committee members will be encouraged instead of the present pattern of confrontation between ruling and opposition parties. We would then see a healthy flow of amendment proposals in committee and debate would also become more accessible to the public, contributing to building the national consensus that is crucial to educational reform.

CONCLUSION

What is needed today is not politicians who are members of Diet cliques specializing in different branches of government administration, but rather politicians who can, in the words of the Constitution, "conduct affairs of state"—politicians capable of overseeing affairs of state as a whole and engaging in comprehensive and strategic policy planning and coordination. The "partial governments" of Diet cliques and individual government agencies are relics of Japan's catching-up period; their persistence is a classic case of an organizational model successful in the past now standing in the way of change. We must not forget that the reform Japan needs to undertake is not only huge in scale but must be accomplished in a limited time. For this reason alone, establishing a cabinet-led system that unifies the ruling party's policy formulation system on the basis of direct election of the prime minister is an urgent task.

The Koizumi cabinet is said to have been formed by means of pseudo-direct election. So far, buoyed by strong public support, it has enjoyed considerable success, including reform of special public corporations and the medical insurance system. But the limits of this approach to reform are also evident. Each reform has required compromise with Diet cliques. Perhaps the clearest evidence of the limits to this approach is the fact that Prime Minister Koizumi himself is urging direct election of the prime minister and unification of policy formulation.

The establishment of a policymaking system suited to pushing through reforms is itself the most critical policy reform needed in Japan today. As the saying goes, the longest way around is the shortest way home.

7

Reform of Corporate Legislation

Ueda Isamu

Since first elected to the House of Representatives in 1993, I have been working in different capacities and with a wide variety of political and policy issues. A major problem that has particularly concerned me in dealing with these issues is the way policy decisions are made. Conventional decision-making processes, including the heavy reliance of the legislative branch of government on the administrative branch (the ministries) and the peculiar symbiosis of politicians and bureaucrats, no longer seem to be effective for the exercise of government at this time of major economic and social transition.

Japan's policymaking system is the subject of numerous studies and discussions that point up both the advantages and disadvantages, so suffice it here to say that, on the whole, it has long worked fairly well within the established framework. And the system has gained respect overseas for having mobilized politicians, bureaucrats, and business leaders in a spirit of cooperation and teamwork.

In the 1980s, while there were signs this system was malfunctioning, the bubble economy generally blocked out evidence of institutional fatigue. As the recession dragged on, however, the inability of politicians, bureaucrats, and businesses to respond to changing times and the resulting sense of deadlock brought the system's endemic problems to the surface.

Various initiatives for reform have been sought since the 1990s in order to break the impasse, but little progress has been made in administrative and economic reform, a situation many observers blame on the bureaucracy's excessive control over policymaking. Calls for stronger political leadership have grown louder. Drastic institutional and policy reforms are needed, but it may be asking too much of the bureaucracy, which is by nature resistant to change, to lead any kind of reform movement. Politicians should take the lead in policymaking initiatives, but the clear outlines of a politician-led government have yet to emerge.

Before entering politics, I worked for the Ministry of Agriculture, Forestry and Fisheries from 1981 to 1992, specializing in infrastructure development projects in rural areas and trade in agricultural, forestry, and fishery products. I observed that the major objective of bureaucrats was simply to maintain the status quo. Though policies might be fine-tuned, I saw that it was impossible to implement major reforms if the initiative was left to bureaucrats. Considering that political leadership would be essential in a time of dramatic change, I decided to become a politician. My studies at the Johnson Graduate School of Management of Cornell University in the United States from 1984 to 1986 also contributed to my skepticism about the workings of the Japanese bureaucracy.

In 1996, I joined the House of Representatives Committee on Judicial Affairs representing the New Frontier Party, which was then among the opposition parties. I remained on the committee for the next five years, although during that time the party with which I was affiliated became part of the ruling coalition. I also served as parliamentary deputy minister of justice for a short period in 2000, during which time a number of amendments were made to corporate legislation and the Commercial Code. I cosponsored, with other Diet members, the bills for some of these amendments. What follows is based on these experiences. Future policymaking and the desirable role of politicians are examined using specific cases of corporate legislation revision. Since I majored in agricultural engineering at university and obtained a master's degree in business administration, I am not an expert in legal affairs. For this reason, the specialist may find the discussion in this chapter problematic in various ways, but I believe my views may be of help from a somewhat different angle.

BACKGROUND OF CORPORATE LEGISLATION

Japanese corporate legislation can be traced back to the Commercial Code established in 1899. Though it has been amended many times since, the text remains written in old-style Japanese. The present legal framework for public corporations is a result of a major revamping of the Commercial Code in 1950. There were further amendments in 1966, 1974,

1981, 1990, 1993, and 1994, although they only partially amended, or supplemented, the basic framework.

Amendments made since 1997 include those resulting from bills introduced by Diet members (table 1). Four amendments were made in 1997, three in 1998, two in 1999, and three in 2000. In 2001, the Diet further liberalized corporate financing by enacting six amendments, including ones originally proposed by Diet members. In addition, as part of bankruptcy-related legislation, the Civil Rehabilitation Law was enacted in 1999, and two amendments to the law were passed in 2000.

INCREASING NEED FOR REVIEW OF CORPORATE LEGISLATION

Until 1993, the Commercial Code was amended mainly to rectify inappropriate business practices, and these amendments were made in response to proposals from parties outside the business community. While amendments were frequently made, designed to promote diversification and smooth the procurement of funds and flexible regulations for small companies, the majority sought more transparent corporate management equipped to deal with such dishonest practices as window dressing of accounts settlements, compensation for trading losses, and the illegal offering of financial benefits to corporate racketeers.

Beginning in the 1980s, Japanese companies were encouraged to rationalize their management as a result of the rapid globalization of the economy and intensifying international competition. Calls for deregulation in corporate law grew louder in the 1990s. Business had been bad as a result of the sluggish domestic economy, so a loosening of government regulations was sought to boost competitiveness. The 1990s saw amendments aimed mainly at the needs of corporate management, but they were not really enough. Nevertheless, structural changes progressed, with a proliferation of mergers and acquisitions, corporate restructuring, and the growth of venture enterprises, as well as changes in employment patterns. As a result of the numerous drastic economic changes, corporate law has frequently been amended since 1997.

However, business leaders feel strongly that Japanese companies cannot compete with their European and American counterparts in the global arena because Western companies operate with fewer restrictions. These leaders have grown increasingly dissatisfied with the slow response of the Ministry of Justice and other government agencies as well as the Diet in tackling this challenge. Economic organizations like Keidanren

Table 1. Amendments to the Civil Rehabilitation Law

Year	Law	Proposer	Purpose
1997	Law for Partial Amendment to the Commercial Code	Diet members	Introduces stock option programs
	Law for Partial Amendment to the Commercial Code		Simplifies procedures for mergers
	Law for Partial Amendment to the Commercial Code		Strengthens regulations to curb the activities of corporate racketeers (*sōkaiya*)
	Law Covering Exceptions to the Commercial Code on the Auditing Practices of Stock Companies, Etc.		
	Law Concerning Exceptions to the Commercial Code on Procedures for Stock Redemption	Diet members	
1998	Law Concerning the Enactment Etc. of Relevant Laws for Reform of the Financial System		
	Law for Partial Amendment to the Law Covering Exceptions to the Commercial Code on the Auditing Practices of Stock Companies, Etc.	Diet members	Expands and extends the law
	Law Concerning Reassessment of Land	Diet members	
1999	Law for Partial Amendment to the Commercial Code Etc.		Simplifies the establishment of complete parent-subsidiary companies
	Law for Partial Amendment to the Law Concerning Reassessment of Land	Diet members	Extends the law
2000	Law for Partial Amendment to the Commercial Code		Establishes a corporate-division system
	Law for Partial Amendment to the Law Concerning Exceptions to the Commercial Code on Procedures for Stock Redemption	Diet members	Expands and extends the law
	Law for Partial Amendment to the Securities and Exchange Law and the Financial Futures Law		

2001	Law for Partial Amendment to the Commercial Code	Diet members	Lifts ban on Treasury stocks, abolishes unit stock system
	Law for Partial Amendment to the Law Concerning Reassessment of Land	Diet members	Expands and extends the law
	Law Concerning Transfer of Short-Term Corporate Bonds, Etc.		Introduces paperless CP
	Law for Partial Amendment to the Law Concerning Safekeeping and Transfer of Stock Certificates		Introduces paperless CP
	Partial Amendment to the Commercial Code		Revises regulations governing stock options and equity issuance; diversifies the range of equity instruments that can be traded (including allow ing tracking of stocks); and recognizes electronic documents as official corporate documents
	Law Covering Exceptions to the Commercial Code on the Auditing Practices of Stock Companies, Etc.	Diet members	Strengthens auditing system and revises regulations governing lawsuits by shareholder representatives

Source: Ueda Eiji et al. 2000. *Heisei shōhō kaisei handobukku* (Heisei-era Commercial Code amendments handbook). Tokyo: Sanseidō.
CP: commercial paper.

(Japan Federation of Economic Organizations) have intensified their pressure on the government and ruling coalition to revise the relevant laws.

In response, the Ministry of Justice started examining this issue in its Legislative Council, an advisory body to the minister of justice, in the fall of 2000. And, with a view to introducing drastic reforms in 2002, the ministry is currently submitting bills to the Diet. Further, it is hoped that the entire text of the Commercial Code will have been rewritten in modern Japanese by fiscal year 2004 (ending March 31, 2005).

AMENDMENT PROCEDURES AND PROBLEMS

The Legislative Council

The Legislative Council of the Ministry of Justice, established in accordance with Article 57 of the Justice Ministry Organization Ordinance, studies and deliberates basic matters concerning civil and criminal law and other legislation as requested by the justice minister. The council examines the bills under the jurisdiction of the ministry and, in principle, even drafts bills. Other government councils can examine basic policy directions and write reports compiling views of their members; only the Justice Ministry's Legislative Council goes as far as to prepare drafts of bills.

The Legislative Council is usually composed of up to 20 members with two-year terms of office. Currently, the council consists of 20 members—scholars of law, judges, lawyers, journalists, and representatives of business organizations and labor unions. Takeshita Morio, president of Surugadai University, is the current chair.

The Legislative Council has seven divisions for deliberation of specific issues by people with professional expertise, namely, the Company Law, Bankruptcy Law, International Jurisdiction System, Warranty-Execution Legislation, Medical Treatment Parent-Child Legislation, and Civil and Personnel Procedure Codes divisions, as well as the Division for the Law Concerning Ownership of Buildings. Each division includes scholars, jurists, journalists, businesspeople, and labor union representatives, all of whom are known for their expertise in their respective areas. Some division members also sit in the Legislative Council, but most are appointed independently of the council. Subcommittees deliberate issues and draft bills, and their reports are brought before a general meeting of the Legislative Council and submitted to the minister for justice after they have received the council's approval. After receiving the reports, the

Ministry of Justice submits the bills, with any minor changes deemed necessary, to the Diet for deliberation.

Assessment of the Legislative Council Approach

Laws under the jurisdiction of the Ministry of Justice are drawn up by a unique process in that the Legislative Council even drafts the text of the bills. Opinion varies concerning this procedure, and its merits (the first three points) and demerits (the second three points) may be summed up as follows.

— Generally, the ministries and agencies hear the views of a wide range of parties in their councils before drafting bills. Under the Ministry of Justice, the Legislative Council, which comprises representatives from various sectors of society, drafts the essential points of the bills, producing a well-balanced product.

— Members with highly specialized knowledge deliberate the details of each bill, which makes it possible to create fine-tuned and reliable legislation. Bills for laws under the jurisdiction of the Ministry of Justice often require particularly cautious examination, because they include not only basic codes for criminal, civil, and commercial law, but also highly technical issues.

— Jurists, businessmen, and labor leaders discuss and adjust differences of opinion in advance, making it less probable that bills will be amended unfairly under undue political pressure after submission to the Diet.

— It takes a long time for bills to be completed because of the time-consuming deliberation by specialists.

— There is little flexibility, since it is difficult to adapt to different situations the conclusions of specialists and representatives of various fields.

— As politicians are rarely involved in drafting legislation, the bills are not written in a format that lends itself to Diet deliberation.

Often, criminal legislation has direct bearing on human rights, and needs to be deliberated widely and carefully. Civil law, too, involves basic legislation bearing on individuals' social standing and property and, therefore, requires thorough discussion. In these cases, where experts attach great importance to diverse and multilayered discussions on legal loopholes and consistency with other laws and ordinances, hypothesizing the various possible applications of the law, the procedure followed by the Ministry of Justice's Legislative Council is most suitable.

In the area of corporate legislation, however, revisions must be made quickly to keep up with the rapidly changing economic conditions. Although precision and reliability are certainly important, the Legislative Council's method of revising legislation is often so slow that the legislation becomes outdated by the time it is approved.

Deregulation of Stock Options

The business world called for the lifting of the ban on the use by venture businesses of stock options as employee incentives, which practice is common in the United States. However, the introduction of stock-option programs was postponed when the Commercial Code was revised in 1994, and was not approved until 1997, when Diet members introduced the requisite legislation. Even so, the law had its limits: stock options were not only limited to board members and company employees, but the options of parent companies could not be offered to board members and employees of subsidiaries. This rule was finally removed in the 2001 extraordinary session of the Diet.

Companies had been banned from acquiring or redeeming their own shares until the Commercial Code was amended in 1994 but, even then, the law stipulated strict conditions. Diet members proposed legislation in 1997 that drastically relaxed these conditions by allowing for there to be "exceptions" to the Commercial Code requirements. Thereafter, Diet members introduced laws that were treated either as exceptions or temporary, so as to relax the regulations concerning the acceptable sources of shares. The main text of the Commercial Code itself was finally amended in the extraordinary Diet sessions in 2001—the bill having been proposed by Diet members—and the ban on companies acquiring and redeeming their own shares was lifted.

The changing of the regulations in the aforementioned two cases was vital if companies were to flexibly finance their operations and corporate management was to become more flexible. Yet the fact that it took a long time for the existing rules to be amended and deregulated shows that existing legislation is not able to keep up with the increasing diversity of corporate activities.

When I studied at business school in the United States, a textbook in one of my basic finance courses explained in detail how this method of acquiring company shares can be a powerful financial tool. Yet it took years for Japan to institute the necessary deregulation. No wonder Japan's corporate law is criticized as being too rigid.

Diet Member Bills and Associated Problems

There are an increasing number of cases in which groups of Diet members have proposed bills for corporate law amendments that are ultimately passed into law. I myself have cosponsored some of them. When the cabinet submits bills to the Diet, the justice minister must consult the Legislative Council, and it often takes years for a conclusion to be reached. When Diet members introduce legislation, consultation with the Legislative Council is not required, substantially cutting down on the time needed for legislation to be passed.

Although discussion and expert input is desirable, the process can be an obstacle when prompt action is needed. However, legislation introduced by Diet members without such deliberation can present problems. Bar associations are generally critical of legislation introduced by politicians because corporate legislation involves numerous technical details, many of which are beyond the expertise of most Diet members.

Given that politicians have to deal with various political and policy issues, there is a limit to which they can follow any one specific issue. As it is difficult to take a broad overall view of the complex and highly technical legal system, politicians inevitably concentrate on the most urgent issues. Laws introduced by politicians are thus often of an emergency nature, being either temporary laws enforced for only a limited period of time, or exceptions relevant to individual cases. Some say that legislator-introduced laws are partial and inconsistent, lacking integrity with the entire legal system. This criticism is difficult to deny.

To compensate for this deficiency, the House of Representatives and the House of Councillors have legislative bureaus and committee research offices. Although the staff of these offices are very capable people, their organizations are not familiar with the intricacies of corporate legislation and so not fully able to deal with specialized and technical issues. Thus Diet members must cooperate with Ministry of Justice officials when they introduce legislation. Officials of this ministry believe that fundamental legislative changes should be handled by groups of experts centering on the justice ministry, and that only those bills addressing major political and social needs should be dealt with by amendments introduced by Diet members. Inevitably, revisions introduced by Diet members will thus be only partial.

Problems of Diet Deliberation

A look at the process of reviewing corporate legislation over the past several years also reveals many problems in the way the Diet deliberates bills.

The passage of bills into law takes a long time, one reason being that the Committees on Judicial Affairs in the House of Representatives and the House of Councillors are extremely slow in examining bills. The committees review corporate, criminal, civil, and immigration-related legislation. Yet, as a rule, they meet only twice a week. During these gatherings, committee members call for explanations from ministers and ministry officials, and the time spent on discussion leaves members little opportunity to examine in depth the bills put before them. Even if the drafting of bills is expedited, it is impossible to shorten the time required for legislation to be passed because of the bottleneck in Diet deliberations.

In addition, politicians and the mass media have little interest in corporate legislation and other areas not closely linked to people's everyday lives. Consequently, much time is spent on bills that are of broad interest to society, and far less on bills that attract little attention. For example, 20 to 30 hours were devoted to deliberating three bills concerning the fight against organized crime, while, due to strong criticism from the opposition, about the same amount of time was spent on a bill to amend the Juvenile Law. Meanwhile, usually less than ten hours are spent deliberating a corporate law amendment.

What is more, since few members of the Committees on Judicial Affairs in the Diet follow particular issues continuously, it is difficult for them to grasp the background and salient features of each issue in a short time. As a result, a few committee members with specialist knowledge will repeatedly take up matters of interest to their supporting organizations, making ideological assertions on their behalf. In reality, few constructive discussions take place in these committee meetings.

Debate on specialist or technically arcane bills, therefore, is often merely a matter of form. Diet judicial affairs committee members are usually faced with processing so many bills that they do not really take part in policymaking. This is true not only in the judicial affairs committees, but also in committees with jurisdiction over industry, finance, the environment, and social security, which issues increasingly require specialized and technical expertise. The problem is most serious with the judicial affairs committees, because they have so many bills to deliberate.

THE DECISION MAKERS

The revision of corporate legislation on the part of politicians, ministry officials, and private sector professionals requires special expertise and prompt policy implementation. Regrettably, however, lawmaking and policy execution do not adequately meet the needs of citizens.

The speed of change in the economic environment of corporate activity continues to accelerate. The development of a global economy has ushered in an era of borderless business and free exchange of both capital and personnel. Capital investment in Japan and mergers and acquisitions of Japanese companies by foreign enterprises are expected to increase rapidly. Corporate law, which can have significant impact on the economy and society, must respond quickly and precisely to these changes and also be in harmony with international rules.

To deal with issues appropriately and quickly, politicians, bureaucrats, and private sector specialists, all of whom differ in position, authority, and capacity, must be aware of their roles and cooperate with each other in a systematic manner. In establishing such relationships, the role played by politicians is the most important.

Politicians

Since politicians daily meet people from many walks of life, they can readily observe the impact of economic changes as well as gauge the need for legislative and/or administrative measures. Ministry officials and private sector specialists, meanwhile, often only have contact with those involved in specific industries. Politicians are familiar with the various views of leaders within the government through their Diet activities and so, being in a position to understand both policymakers and those demanding change, they are well placed to coordinate conflicting interests.

Although Diet members have the right to investigate and are responsible for all matters of national government, there is a limit to the influence a politician can have on policy decision making. Therefore, policy decisions are often first made at the party level, through discussions within politicians' respective parties, and a majority opinion is formed in the Diet by approaching other parties and politicians. But because of the rapid pace of social change and the increasingly specialized nature of issues, it is difficult for political parties to deliberate issues in depth. Among individual lawmakers, discussions tend to be affected by the media and pressure from interest groups. Decisions are often left up to the directors of divisions and executive members of committees, who follow pet issues and maintain contact with the parties concerned. In many cases, they demonstrate wise policy judgment. For issues that attract strong interest or that are fundamental to the ruling of the nation, it is increasingly necessary to reach a consensus within each political party, which in turn helps promote people's understanding of issues through the mass media. However, it appears the role and the capability of political parties in deciding individual policies has weakened. Now that no party holds a secure, absolute majority in the Diet and coalition government is the norm, Diet members who share similar views generally make nonpartisan decisions reflecting the governing parties' views.

In order to do so, politicians must fully understand the background, interests, and international assessment of individual issues and policies that the cabinet aims to achieve. They must concentrate on specific policies for a time, while maintaining communication with government officials and others concerned. The *zoku* or groupings of Diet members that represent the interests and opinions of specific alliances are harshly criticized today, but legislators do need in-depth expertise on certain issues and, as long as they do not distort policy decisions to benefit specific interest groups, their communication with such alliances need not necessarily be censured.

Politicians are not expected to have as much detailed knowledge as bureaucrats, scholars, or private sector experts, although they must make proper judgments on national policies in specific areas and have an adequate level of knowledge and understanding to coordinate the opinions of various interest groups. More importantly, however, they should have insight into both the basic policies of the government and international affairs.

Senior Vice Ministers and Parliamentary Secretaries

In the Japanese parliamentary system, ministers, senior vice ministers, and parliamentary secretaries play important roles. They are selected from among lawmakers and are directly involved in and responsible for policy decisions and their implementation. The system of senior vice ministers and parliamentary secretaries was established in January 2001 in response to the criticism that ministers depended too much on input solely from the officials of their respective ministries and agencies.

Representing their ministries and agencies, ministers are responsible for policy as a whole and are so busy that they cannot become directly involved in specific and specialized policy issues. Senior vice ministers and parliamentary secretaries are expected, therefore, to coordinate the opinions of bureaucrats, private sector experts, and other concerned parties, integrate those opinions with cabinet policies, and come up with a relevant agenda for each ministry. Since senior vice ministers and parliamentary secretaries are sensitive to the various needs of the people, they can prevent bureaucrats, who often hear the voices of only a limited number of interest groups, from employing self-serving measures detrimental to the nation.

In addition, they are expected to play a major role in coordinating opinion in the Diet and among political parties; indirectly support and coordinate Diet deliberations on bills and discussions within parties; as well as communicate with both their counterparts in other ministries and agencies when issues overlap, and ruling and opposition party members in charge of policy.

I served as parliamentary vice minister in the Ministry of Justice in the second half of 2000, immediately before the ministerial reorganization. Besides the minister, the parliamentary vice minister was the only lawmaker appointed to serve in a ministry, and I found it impossible to take part in every policy discussion. While the minister was busy dealing with questions in the Diet and attending official functions, I was involved in discussion with political parties on the details of bills and coordination of their Diet activities. Based on this experience, I felt that at least three lawmakers should be assigned to each ministry to take senior vice minister or parliamentary secretary posts, so that they might be involved in each policy area at a more specialist level. This practice was, in fact, introduced in January 2001.

For this system to function well, the right people must be appointed to positions appropriately reflecting their expertise, and their term in office should be at least two years. I had not been directly involved in judicial administration before I was appointed parliamentary vice minister in the Ministry of Justice, but had served in posts as a director and/or member of the House of Representatives Committee for Judicial Affairs for about five years. Because of this experience, I had a basic understanding of the content, background, and priorities of the ministry's policies. That enabled me to take part in the making and implementation of policy decisions immediately after my appointment. Had I lacked experience in judicial issues, it would have taken me a long time to develop a basic understanding. Yet, since I left my post after just six months, I had to drop most of the issues I had started to tackle.

Regrettably, the new system of senior vice ministers and parliamentary secretaries is not being fully utilized by the cabinet under the Koizumi

Jun'ichirō administration. Instead, it is increasing the number of people working in the cabinet secretariat and using specialists from the private sector, thereby augmenting the capability of basic policymaking, and formulating many new policies for economic management and administrative reform. I have a high opinion of the Koizumi cabinet because it is less dependent on bureaucrats and, under the prime minister's leadership, has broken down the stratification of each ministry and agency, and come up with bold reform measures. However, the cabinet secretariat's staff is not enough to adequately implement policy measures, especially those involving a wide range of technical information. The key to establishing true political leadership is to allow the appointed senior vice ministers and parliamentary secretaries to fulfill their mission.

Bureaucrats

The staff of government ministries have an in-depth understanding of very specific policy areas due to their many years' work in the bureaucracy. Many competent officials deal with issues systematically and their organizations excel in gathering and analyzing information. The role of bureaucrats, therefore, is particularly important in a highly technical policy area such as corporate legislation.

In the course of their work, however, bureaucrats have frequent contact with specific interest groups, so there is a risk that these groups may unduly influence their making and implementation of policies. With regard to corporate law, Ministry of Justice officials spend enormous amounts of time with law scholars, judges, and lawyers whose views tend to be reflected strongly in legislation. At the same time, the views or practical expertise of business executives, managers, and related interest groups are often slighted.

Bureaucrats tend to attach great importance to the continuity and consistency of policy, preferring to follow precedent. They are also criticized for their tendency to focus excessively on details and to lack a broader perspective, which inclination stems from their specialist knowledge and access to detailed information.

Bureaucrats should provide professional and technical advice to their ministers, senior vice ministers, and parliamentary secretaries so that the politicians appointed to serve in their ministries can make appropriate judgments. Government officials should also have sufficient professional knowledge and experience to carry out wise policy decisions, for their role in drawing up and implementing policies is crucial.

Opposition Politicians

Opposition parties also have an extremely important role to play in government policymaking. Given the need to deal expeditiously with the making and implementation of policy in this age of rapid change, the government and the ruling parties cannot pay enough attention to the interests and views of the various groups concerned, which increases the risk of biased judgments. Since politicians have contact with people in all walks of life, putting them in a position to readily gauge legislative and administrative responses to the people's needs, they should consider policy issues and problems from perspectives other than those of ruling party politicians and bureaucrats.

In the area of corporate law, while amendments are made in response to requests from the business world, the views of labor unions, management and employees of small and medium-sized enterprises, as well as lawyers, accountants, tax accountants, and other specialists should also be taken into account. Diet members from the ruling parties should try to accommodate differences as much as possible, but opposition lawmakers should present perspectives that ruling politicians may lack, make constructive criticisms, and offer policy proposals from a different standpoint in a sustained and systematic manner.

For policy planning and proposals, the ruling parties can expect the support of bureaucrats, but opposition parties must rely on their own politicians and the small staffs of Diet secretariat officials. This makes it difficult for the opposition to present specific policy proposals that require special expertise and continual involvement, often enabling it to do little more than criticize bills submitted by the government and ruling parties.

If political leadership is to become more dynamic, the opposition parties must play a more active and constructive role: The shortages of personnel and resources in their parties and the Diet secretariat must be resolved and full use must be made of private sector think tanks and nonprofit organizations (NPOs). This would allow surveys and research to be conducted on policy issues from perspectives other than those of the government and ruling coalition.

Diet Secretariat Staff, Think Tanks, and NPOs

There are many talented people in the Diet secretariat, as well as scholars, researchers, businesspeople, lawyers, and others with more professional expertise than bureaucrats.

Although lawmakers depend mainly on bureaucrats for specialized information, greater participation by other elements would add dynamism to policymaking, rendering it more responsive to the needs of the public.

To this end, it must be made possible to undertake policy surveys and research from a relatively stable position, which would require the recruiting of scholars and private sector personnel to work in the Diet's legislative bureaus and committee research offices. This would necessitate diversified employment conditions allowing fixed-term employment and the holding of other jobs concurrently. There should also be a recruitment system encouraging employment of talented and diverse personnel as policy secretaries to Diet members and policy officers in political parties.

The services of some private sector think tanks and NPOs that conduct policy research and compile recommendations are already being tapped. The Basic Design for Reform of the Civil Servant System, a policy adopted by the Cabinet Headquarters for Administrative Reform on June 29, 2001, proposes that private sector personnel be recruited as administrative officers, the exchange of public and private sector personnel be promoted, a national strategy staff comprising bureaucrats and nonbureaucrats be created, and ministers' support staff be increased. Such changes would allow capable personnel from private sector think tanks and NPOs to help draft and implement policy.

To benefit from the talents of policy-oriented personnel with fresh ideas, it must be made easier for staff to move among government, private sector, and university posts. In the United States, there are many nonprofit private think tanks in which those competent enough to take important posts in the legislative and executive branches of government can undertake research activities relatively freely when they leave those posts. Given Japan's different personnel management system, think tanks as large as those in the United States may not be required, but Japanese think tanks do, nevertheless, need to increase in number and size. In the United States, think tanks are mostly funded by companies and individuals. To encourage similar support in Japan would require the expansion and simplification of preferential tax regulations that currently apply exclusively to specific public-interest promotion corporations and particular nonprofit corporations.

Power shifts and realignments among political parties, as well as changes in the makeup of the ruling coalition are quite possible in Japan's current political climate: A party in the opposition today may become a ruling party tomorrow. It is thus important that opposition parties improve their policymaking skills so that when they become a ruling party, those individuals from think tanks and NPOs who have helped them with policymaking can play an active role as staff in the government's state strategy programs or in the offices of cabinet ministers.

POLICY DECISION MAKING IN THE FUTURE

A New System Led by Legislator Initiative

Some of the problems in Japan's policy decision process can be understood by focusing on highly technical corporate legislation that has a powerful impact on the economy. Traditionally, politicians left to the bureaucrats such policy areas as corporate law. However, this system is no longer functioning properly and must be replaced by one in which lawmakers are the major players. To this end, complementary relations must be established among politicians, bureaucrats, and private sector experts, and should be coordinated by politicians who should play a major role in shaping policy. There need be no confrontation with bureaucrats as the politicians keep tabs on the trends of the times and changing circumstances so as to have a sufficient grasp of sophisticated policy issues to enable them to persuade others.

Institutional Reform

To introduce and firmly establish a new decision-making system driven by lawmaker initiative, there need to be a number of institutional reforms, to which end the following steps should be taken.

First, greater importance should be attached to the selection of senior vice ministers and parliamentary secretaries, taking into account aptitude and experience, and terms of office should be secured for at least one to two years.

Second, staff for ministers and senior vice ministers should be recruited from inside and outside the administration, transcending the boundaries among ministries/agencies and regardless of civil service rank. A wide range of private sector experts should also be recruited from think tanks and NPOs.

Third, the budget for Diet staff and their numerical quota should be increased to enable private sector experts to participate in research and lawmaking programs in the legislative branch of government. To encourage their recruitment, it is necessary to study the possibility of issue-based, fixed-term contracts, and a relaxation of regulations on holding other jobs concurrently.

Fourth, expanding government support for personnel expenses should be examined so that politicians can recruit the most capable staff.

Fifth, preferential taxation and other effective measures must be instituted to encourage the growth of private sector think tanks and NPOs, which are the source of future policy staff.

Sixth, personnel mobility must be ensured so that competent people can exercise their talents in various positions and develop their expertise. To this end, government offices and private companies must drastically change their approach to personnel management, while the social security system must be reviewed accordingly.

Seventh, to encourage more lively deliberation in Diet committees, (1) committee meetings should convene more flexibly; (2) opportunities for an open exchange of views in subcommittees and panel meetings should supplement the standard deliberations in which committee members ask questions of the government, so that the details of the text of bills can be discussed and multiple themes can be debated simultaneously; and (3) the requirement that ministers and senior vice ministers attend committee meetings should be more flexibly applied.

Finally, the practice—already a mere formality—of giving reasons for proposals and party representatives' questions in the plenary sessions of the Diet should be abolished, except concerning the prime minister's policy speech and budget bills. In addition, a system should be set up in which ministers who do not have direct jurisdiction over issues being discussed can attend committee meetings as deemed necessary by the relevant committees.

About the Contributors

Gerald L. Curtis is Burgess Professor of Political Science at Columbia University and Visiting Professor at the Graduate Institute for Policy Studies in Tokyo. He is the author of numerous books on Japanese politics, U.S.-Japan relations, and U.S. policy in East Asia. These include *The Logic of Japanese Politics*, which draws on his intimate knowledge of the personalities that have dominated Japan's political landscape for the past 30 years, and *The Japanese Way of Politics*, for which he was awarded the Masayoshi Ōhira Memorial Prize. His book and articles have been published in Japanese, Chinese, Korean, Thai, French, and other languages. Professor Curtis is advisor and monthly columnist for the *Chūnichi/Tokyo Shimbun* and Special Advisor to *Newsweek* for *Newsweek* Japan and *Newsweek* Korea. He is a member of the Board of Directors of the United States-Japan Foundation, the Board of Directors of the Japan Center for International Exchange, Inc. (USA), the Advisory Board to the National Institute for Democracy, the Advisory Board to the Foundation for Advanced Information and Research (FAIR), and the Editorial Board of the journal *Asian Survey*.

Furukawa Motohisa is serving his second term as a Democratic Party of Japan (DPJ) Member of the House of Representatives and is the Deputy Chair of the DPJ's Public Relations Committee. Educated at the University of Tokyo and Columbia University, he joined the Ministry of Finance in 1988 and held various positions, including chief of the Planning Section and chief of the Securities and Banking Inspection and Surveillance System Investigation Division. In 1996, he was first elected to the House of

Representatives and became vice president of the DPJ's Policy Research Committee. Within the House of Representatives, he is a director of the Committee on Financial Affairs.

Hase Hiroshi is a Liberal Democratic Party (LDP) Member of the House of Representatives. After graduation from Senshū University in 1984, Mr. Hase became a Japanese teacher at his high school alma mater, Seiryō High School. In 1984 he participated in the Los Angeles Olympic games as an amateur wrestler, and turned professional the following year by joining Japan Pro-Wrestling. In 1995, he was elected to the House of Councillors from Ishikawa Prefecture with support from the LDP and subsequently joined the LDP. In 2000, he was elected a member of the House of Representatives. Within the House of Representatives, he is a director of the Committee on Rules and Administration; a member of the Committee on Education, Culture, Sports, Science and Technology; and a member of the Deliberative Council on Political Ethics. Within the LDP, he is a member of the Policy Deliberation Commission and deputy director of the following divisions within the Policy Research Council: Environment Division; Land, Infrastructure and Transport Division; and Health, Labor and Welfare Division.

Itō Tatsuya is serving his third term as a Liberal Democratic Party (LDP) Member of the House of Representatives. A graduate of Keiō University's Faculty of Law in 1984, Mr. Itō studied at the Matsushita Institute of Government and Management. He was a visiting scholar at the Graduate Program in Public Policy and Administration at California State University, Sacramento, while serving as a policy staff member of the office of the Mayor of Sacramento City from 1987 to 1988. After returning to Japan in 1988, he founded the Brain 21 Institute and served as the Executive Director of the U.S.-Japan Technology Exchange Council (Alliance 90). He was first elected to the House of Representatives in 1993. In the House of Representatives, he is currently a director of the Committee on Economy, Trade and Industry, and a member of the Research Commission on the Constitution. Within the LDP, he serves as director of the Economy, Trade and Industry Division of the Policy Research Council; director general, Special Committee on e-Japan; and director, Administrative Reform Promotion Headquarters.

Maehara Seiji is serving his third term as a Democratic Party of Japan (DPJ) Member of the House of Representatives. He is deputy secretary-general of the DPJ. After graduating from the University of Kyoto's Faculty of Law in 1988, Mr. Maehara joined the Matsushita Institute of Government and Management where he conducted research on various policy issues. In 1991, he was elected to the Kyoto Prefectural Assembly and in 1993 he joined the Japan New Party upon its establishment. He was elected to the House in 1993 from the Kyoto First District and was reelected in 1996 from the Kinki Proportional Representation District. He joined the New Party Sakigake in 1994, and later joined the DPJ at the time of its foundation in 1996. He is currently a member of the House Committee on Land, Infrastructure and Transport and the House Committee on Security.

Nemoto Takumi is serving his third term as a Liberal Democratic Party (LDP) Member of the House of Representatives and is former State Secretary for Health and Welfare (1998–1999) under the Obuchi Cabinet. After graduating from the University of Tokyo, he joined the Ministry of Construction in 1974. In 1993, he was first elected to the House of Representatives, and was reelected in 1996 and 2000. He is currently a director of the House Committee on Financial Affairs and a member of the Committee on Economy, Trade and Industry. Within the LDP, he is acting director of the Treasury and Finance Division and deputy director of the Health, Labor and Welfare Division of the Policy Research Council; deputy chairman of the Special Committee on the Promotion of a Total Plan for Financial Reconstruction; deputy director of the Administrative Reform Promotion Headquarters; and director of the Research Commission on the Tax System.

Ueda Isamu is serving his third term as a New Kōmeitō Member of the House of Representatives. After graduating from the University of Tokyo's Faculty of Agriculture, he joined the Ministry of Agriculture, Forestry and Fisheries in 1981. Mr. Ueda was elected to the House of Representatives in 1993, and reelected in 1996 and 2000. He was initially a member of the Kōmeitō Party, and joined the New Frontier Party in 1994 upon its establishment and participated in the establishment of the New Peace Party in 1998. In 2000, he was senior state secretary for justice. He is a director of the Committee on Foreign Affairs, member of the Committee on Financial Affairs, and member of the Special Committee on Prevention of International Terrorism and Japan's Cooperation and Support in the

House of Representatives. Within the New Kōmeitō Party, he is assistant secretary general and chairman of the Committee for Foreign Affairs and Security in the Policy Council. He received his M.B.A. in 1986 from Cornell University's Johnson Graduate School of Management.

Index

The Japan Center for International Exchange

Founded in 1970, the Japan Center for International Exchange (JCIE) is an independent, nonprofit, and nonpartisan organization dedicated to strengthening Japan's role in international affairs. JCIE believes that Japan faces a major challenge in augmenting its positive contributions to the international community, in keeping with its position as one of the world's largest industrial democracies. Operating in a country where policymaking has traditionally been dominated by the government bureaucracy, JCIE has played an important role in broadening debate on Japan's international responsibilities by conducting international and cross-sectional programs of exchange, research, and discussion.

JCIE creates opportunities for informed policy discussions; it does not take policy positions. JCIE programs are carried out with the collaboration and cosponsorship of many organizations. The contacts developed through these working relationships are crucial to JCIE's efforts to increase the number of Japanese from the private sector engaged in meaningful policy research and dialogue with overseas counterparts.

JCIE receives no government subsidies; rather, funding comes from private foundation grants, corporate contributions, and contracts.